Loving Men

Loving Men

Gay Partners, Spirituality, and AIDS

Richard P. Hardy

CONTINUUM • NEW YORK

1998

The Continuum Publishing Company
370 Lexington Avenue, New York, NY 10017

Copyright © 1998 by Richard P. Hardy

Printed in the United States of America

Library of Congress Cataloging-in-Publication Data
Hardy, Richard P.
    Loving men : gay partners, spirituality, and AIDS / Richard P. Hardy.
        p.   cm.
    Includes bibliographical references.
    ISBN 0-8264-1138-X
    1. AIDS (Disease) – Religious aspects – Christianity. 2. AIDS (Disease) – Religious aspects. 3. Gay male couples – United States. 4. Gay male couples – Canada. 5. Gay men – Religious life. 6. Gay men – Interviews.   I. Title.
    BV4910.3.H37   1998
    261.8'7662 – dc21   98-20737

To Yoshio
and all the partners
who give life through their deep love
with all its passion and gentleness

Contents

Introduction

A Beginning

Every person has a story, and all that it contains forms part of humanity's history. Moreover, the person's unique story is a sacred place which gives birth to spirituality. Unspoken, the richness of its contribution to human history and spirituality remains unknown. For centuries societies refused to include the stories of countless gay persons, thus impoverishing our history. This book hopes to provide the opportunity for the enrichment of history and spirituality as it presents the stories of various gay men who lived in loving relationships and in so doing created a spirituality. The partners in this book agreed to tell their stories and claim them as their own living mark in humanity's journey toward humanization. In various ways, they understood that this process, while good for them, was not something they could jealously guard and keep for themselves. The love they had been given and shared with their lovers challenged them to offer it as a hope to others. It was something precious to them. Only their sense of its giftedness would allow them to claim it and to offer it to others. Accepting to share their story in words, they wanted others to find the mystery not only in their lives, but in the lives that the listeners and readers themselves experienced.

During the process of research and interviewing the various partners, very often I found myself feeling like a child sitting at the feet of Wisdom personified and hearing what life and love offered to all. I was on sacred ground, a sacred ground which I had no absolute right to enter. Entering it was a gift which each of these gay men granted me and others who would hear their stories. And I was grateful. As the interviews continued, I became more and more aware of the profound importance of each story for our time. I became convinced of the absolute necessity of others hearing these stories of suffering, joy, hope, strength, fear, love, anger, and peace.

As a gay man who lost a partner due to complications from AIDS, I could resonate with much of the experience of the men I interviewed in the process of gathering material for this book. The very fact that I too have a story means that there would be advantages as well as disadvantages as I wrote this book. My experience could perhaps enable me to understand more fully than one who has not had the experience of living with and loving one who lived with HIV/AIDS. The resonances struck within me and I could listen with more than my ears alone because of the common bond of the experience. Yet, at the same time, I realized that I had to be aware that my experience might color what I was hearing. This meant that I had to be particularly astute as I listened to the individuals and their stories unfolding before me. Furthermore, in the process of writing, I knew that it was necessary to allow these men to narrate their own journeys with each of the particularities they involved.

Yet, anyone who writes does so from the perspective of the self that one is discovering over one's own lifetime. It is this stance that makes any writing alive and authentic. Even the most demanding researcher of "objective science" can never remain totally aloof or objective. One need look only at the historian to see this. So in this sense the pages which follow are not meant to be a purely objective study, nor could they be.

While presenting the story as these partners told it, I attempted to listen, read, and imbibe it within the context of the self that I am becoming. What I speak of here is the understanding I have and the hope I have for human life to become more human, humane, and compassionate; these are also the special stories of the journeys of these gay men who loved in a time of HIV/AIDS. I hope I have done justice to them.

The gay men I interviewed as the basis for this book came from various cities in Canada and the United States. Some of the men who agreed to share their stories were people I knew personally. Others came to me through persons who knew of my research and who had informed them about it. These latter contacted me or told the person to have me call them because they wanted to participate. The group consisted of English- and French-speaking men, Native peoples of Canada, men of Asian and Pacific Islander backgrounds, as well as Caucasian men. Some retained a connection with an institutional church — usually the Metropolitan Community Church (MCC) or the Episcopal Church. The majority had left the institutional churches (and in the case of one participant, the synagogue) of their youth. Most maintained a faith in God, however they would name that God. Some were agnostic. Almost all gave me permission to use their real names. However, for various reasons, including a certain consistency in writing, I have given each one a pseudonym. The partners whom they loved also have fictitious names.

Many had been members of the Roman Catholic Church. It is clear that the official statements of this church, and of many other Christian churches, have not been favorable to their gay and lesbian members despite the individual priests or ministers who have journeyed with us with great understanding and compassion. Because of the official stances, many gay men have had to choose between remaining members of these churches and their own integrity and development as human beings. Such a choice should not have to be made in order to be an authentic Christian, but it has been and still is the case for many gay men.

As gay men we belong to a part of society that some others would prefer not to see exist. We are gay. We are lovers. We are partners. We are celibates. We are single. We are physicians, construction workers, professors, lawyers, ministers, carpenters, priests, rabbis, artists, clerks, restauranteurs, chaplains, as well as belonging to a host of other professions in every segment of society. This book tells the stories of some of us: our love, our hopes, our joys, our despairs, our dreams, our pain, our sorrow, our grieving. But above all, it is the story of who we are and have dared to be in the face of hatred, violence, and isolation. We are and we will be there always. The men who agreed to be interviewed and have their stories told wanted others to know of the love which existed in their lives; but more especially they wanted others to know that such deep love was possible. HIV/AIDS has not destroyed their love. Rather it has made them ever more deeply aware of the fact that whatever others might say of them, they were ordinary people who lived ordinary lives in love, concern, and compassion.

Before 1990, only one published book dealt with the experiences of partners whose lovers lived with HIV/AIDS. This was written by Paul Monette. While on a plane traveling to Hong Kong to give some lectures, I began reading Monette's *Borrowed Time: An AIDS Memoir.*[1] I could not put it down. His superb writing skills and what he said captivated me. Later I read his short book of poems, which speak of his own feelings as he reflected on his relationship with his lover, especially during the time after his lover's death.[2]

Gradually, more published material on partners came out. Two collections of AIDS stories were published in 1992. In Joe Brown,

ed., *A Promise to Remember: The Names Project Book of Letters: Remembrances from the Contributors to the Quilt*,[3] and Neal
Hitchens, *Voices That Care: Stories and Encouragements for People
with AIDS/HIV and Those Who Love Them*,[4] one finds a few rec-
ollections of surviving partners. In the same year, R. Dennis Shelby
published his excellent psychological study drawn from his experience of counseling gay men in relationships in the context of AIDS.[5]
Robert J. L. Publicover's memoir as a partner, *My Unicorn Has
Gone Away: Life, Death, Grief, and Living in the Years of AIDS*,
was also published in 1992.[6]

Finally, in 1996 we find two superb books written as partners'
memoirs. Both these rank, in my opinion, as milestones of literary
and reflective pieces along with Monette's work, as they detail the
authors' relationships with their lovers who died of complications
from AIDS. They are Mark Doty's *Heaven's Coast: A Memoir* and
Fenton Johnson's *Geography of the Heart: A Memoir*.[7]

There are many who have assisted me in a variety of ways as I
set out to do the research and to write this book. Among them,
I wish to give a special thanks to Dr. William Lindsey, whose ed-
itorial work and superb suggestions made this book possible. The
suggestions of Frank Oveis of Continuum Publishing Group enabled
me to make the text more readable. I would also like to thank all
those who supported and encouraged me in so many ways, especially: Professor Dennis Haubrich; the Research Center of Saint Paul
University, Ottawa; James Roche; the people of the Living Room of
the AIDS Committee of Ottawa; Claudette Gravelle, S.G.O.; Eleanor
Monahan, C.N.D.; the Reverend Alan Eddington; the Metropolitan
Community Church of San Francisco; Robert Doran, S.J.; Thomas
Hayes, O.M.I.; David Hoe; Professor L. William Countryman; Caryl
Green; Professor Hubert Doucet; Professor Kenneth Melchin; Pro-
fessor David Perrin, O.M.I.; Professor J. Michael Clark; Professor
Michael L. Stemmeler; David Rimmer; Brother Antonio Sarto, S.F.;
Rev. Canon Fran Tornquist; Lisa Capaldini, M.D.; Noriko Obi-
nata; Professor Tom West, O.F.M.; Professor William Short, O.F.M.;
Yukihiro Yasuda and Vince Crisostomo of Asian & Pacific Islander
Wellness Center, San Francisco; the Reverend Peter V. Hayn; and my
former students at Saint Paul University. Those who offered to share
their stories as partners of persons living with HIV/AIDS, without
whose selfless opening of their lives this book would not have been

possible, have my deepest thanks. You know who you are and I am more than grateful to you all. Yoshio, who kept encouraging me to write this book when I became discouraged about ever being able to finish it, deserves much thanks. His love and support as well as his playfulness were just what I needed over the three years I worked on it. My memories of the short time Hiro and I spent together provided me with the impetus to go on and complete it.

To all of them and to those who have already shared their stories as partners, I am grateful.

Chapter 1

Spirituality:
Journey of the Enfleshed Life

As we look at various segments of our society, we discover that there is a deepening hunger for meaning in life. More often than not people seek that meaning in what they call spirituality. Recently, as I walked through the Castro in San Francisco, I was struck by the number of times I heard people talking about spirituality, meaning, and life. While waiting for the bus on Market Street, I overheard two men talking about wanting more than just one-night stands. They spoke of how they wanted their sexual intimacy to be based on a meaningful friendship. At a coffee shop on Eighteenth Street, two others were engrossed in a discussion on what spirituality was and how it could be developed. Another gay man spoke of the need to renew himself through getting in touch with his inner self. A group meets monthly to talk about spirituality and their lives as gay men. These gay men might be in the minority in the gay community, but there is no doubt that spirituality is increasingly becoming an important element in the lives of gay men, even those who remain in the "spirituality closet." Let's face it, in some circles in the gay community it is not politically correct to discuss spirituality.

There may be many reasons for this closetedness about spirituality. One of the most likely is that spirituality is so often associated in the ordinary person's mind with religion. Having suffered so much oppression and rejection by various religious communities, gay men and lesbians very often reject not only religion but spirituality as well because they identify the two. Yet, that identification is breaking down for gay people.

In a recent issue of *San Francisco Frontiers*, Kate Kendell spoke of her growing up in the Mormon Church and the conflict that arose within her as a result of affirming her own lesbianism as well as her feminist development:

Now, after years of being confidently and rather rigidly in-different to all things religious or spiritual, I am finally acknowledging that, for me, there is something missing. Perhaps I can recognize that without feeling I'm betraying my agnostic leanings. Perhaps my complete distrust in organized religion has lifted just enough for me to see that there is a difference between spirituality and religion.[8]

As executive director of the National Center for Lesbian Rights, she reflects on the need and desire she has for a spiritual component to her life, a component that will enhance her life as a whole. Religion, she notes, has failed in what it was meant to do: bring love and remove hatred, ignorance, and violence. As she and other lesbians and gay men are discovering the difference between religion and spirituality, they discover a freedom to choose a spirituality which empowers them to live fully as human beings.[9]

A False Dualism

Yet, other obstacles exist for gay people who might want to investigate the possibility of finding a spirituality which could deepen their lives. Like most people in North America, gay people often think of spirituality as something disincarnate, that is, having nothing to do with the flesh, the body. To be spiritual is often seen as something which denies the body and the flesh or at the very most has nothing to do with our physical being. Evidently, such an approach seems totally against the rediscovery and revaluing of the body which the gay community rightly advocates. From Stonewall onward, many gay men tried to reconstruct a community that valued the body and the pleasures it could offer. Some, however, fell into the old dualism, but this time downplaying the essential element of *spirit*. If we are to be truly human, we must affirm the whole person rather than try to be just a body or just a spirit.

We all suffer from the historical developments of a spirituality which became corrupted by a dualism which separated body and spirit. The root of the word "spirituality" is *spiritus,* meaning life or breath. It denotes a healthy lifestyle of wholeness. However, by the twelfth century "spirituality" came to mean the opposite of materiality and even the opposite of one's day-to-day material and bodily existence.[10] This created a body-spirit split. As a result, most people perceived the "spiritual" and "spirituality" as having nothing to do with the body. In fact, people often saw spirituality not only as different from body and the world but, consonant with their internalized dualism, in opposition to it. Moreover, religious groups thought trying to live as a disembodied soul was the primary goal of one's existence. Bodily life and the world were things to be avoided as much as possible. One's whole life therefore was meant to be lived as a *fuga mundi*, a flight from the world and anything bodily. Such approaches maintained that as human beings we were meant to live here in exile awaiting death when we could finally attain our real goal and only real home: eternity as spirits.[11] Such a dualism, which created the opposition of body and soul, spirit and matter, established classes of *holy* people: clergy and religious women were first class because — at least in theory — they had renounced the world and the body while living here; ordinary lay women and men who had to be concerned about things of the body and the world were merely second class. Such views brought about by this dichotomy pervaded religious life throughout the centuries. It even remains part of our own times, for many people in the Christian tradition still think about spirituality — and indeed Christian existence — in this way.

Spirituality: Affirming Life and Body

It is no wonder that the majority of Christian institutions view gay men who affirm their sexuality and live out their bodiliness as having no spirituality at all. It is not only homophobia that produces their condemnation of gay men and our so-called lifestyle. It is the effect of the interaction of both homophobia and some Christian churches' teachings which foster the idea that gay men and lesbians cannot live a spirituality. Furthermore, when gay persons come out and affirm who they are as good and that loving as gay persons is good, it is no wonder that they often reject any notion of spirituality as conceived in this dualistic tradition. For they have not only internalized the homophobia present in society, but they have also internalized that false view of spirituality.

Spirituality in its best sense affirms life, the body, and the world as well as the transcendent dimension in human life. It is not something that removes us from life but enfleshes us ever more in relationship to each other, the world, and the Transcendent, whether seen as primary value or God. Spirituality here includes an essential part of human life: one's sexuality, which pervades the whole of any person's being. Making love becomes one of the highest forms of the integrating process of spirituality. An authentic spirituality not only

roots us in life; it enhances our bodiliness as the only possible way
to develop spirituality and to live it.[12]

Such a view of spirituality opens possibilities for life enhancement for gay men and especially for gay men whose partners live
with HIV/AIDS. Our identities as gay men include our sexuality
as an essential component. To find a spirituality that not only allows for sexuality and genital expression, but affirms its importance
in human development creates entirely new possibilities for our enfleshed living. Indeed, our nonconformity to the heterosexist norm
for sexuality contributes not only to our own construction of gay religious identity,[13] but provides the opportunity for the reconstruction
of a healthier, wholesome heterosexuality for others. From the margins, we as gay men who strive to live an authentic spirituality can
teach the heterosexual majority what it means to be truly human.[14]
Spirituality is at the very heart of being human.

Moreover, spirituality for the human being takes on a variety of
possibilities of expression. It can be humanist as well as religious. As
I use the term, humanist spirituality can be nontheistic (agnostic or
atheist) or theistic (either drawing from a previously held religious
tradition or totally separated from one, though still theistic). Religious spirituality, and in this case Christian spirituality, involves a
relationship with the God made known in Jesus Christ through the
Spirit along with membership in one of the institutional forms of
Christianity. Let us examine in more detail what we mean by these
various types or expressions of spirituality.

Humanist Spirituality

Many members of organized religion cannot envision the possibility of an authentic spirituality existing outside of a church. For
such people, a *real* spirituality could never be nontheistic, much
less atheistic, or even one separate from religion. Many gay men
and nonreligious people hold this view resulting from our Western
Christian culture in which there is such a strong identification of
spirituality and organized religion. For them, the very word *spirituality* raises a red flag because of their negative and condemnatory
experiences in religious institutions they decided to leave long ago as
obstacles to becoming fully human.

Yet, even in those who reject a religious spirituality, often we find
a life lived in a developing wholeness. Each one finds within his own
story a way of living in relationship to others and the world. The

memoirs of two men writing of their love and loss of their partner contain the undercurrent of their spirituality — for their stories are their spirituality. Mark Doty in *Heaven's Coast: A Memoir* gives us a poignant description of the process of losing his lover:

> What was can't be restored; I can neither have Wally back in the flesh, nor return to the self I inhabited before his death. The vessel's not cracked but broken, all the way through, permanently. . . . But who can live, day by day, in pieces? Loss shatters us, first, but then what? . . . Broken, ongoing, we see at once what it was and what it is. Wearing its history, the old cup with its gilt scars becomes, I imagine, a treasure of another sort, whole in its own fragmentation, more deeply itself, veined with the evidence of time.[15]

Facing death and the loss of one's partner in life must not be suppressed. Only living it fully and thereby coming to a kind of peace with it empowers one to live and that is what matters.

Another lover, Fenton Johnson, experiencing such loss says this:

> To be spared complacency, or shocked from it — this is no small gift; however, its price may be unbearably high. To live with that intensity is a brilliant thing. . . . Whether their particular trauma makes headlines is irrelevant — the whole fate of humanity expresses itself in each of our deaths. What is of consequence is how we live — how we arrive at our deaths; what we make with what we have been given.[16]

As each of us lives life consciously with all that it contains of joy and horror and banality, we are involved in seeking and living out a meaning. This process is spirituality in its truest sense.

These two men with their extraordinary ability to express their stories narrate their spirituality. In a humanist sense, "being spiritual is an attribute of the way one experiences the world and lives one's life."[17] Yet it is more than just going through life. Life's experiences become spiritual when they are consciously seen and lived as a part of a world and therefore a meaning which is larger than themselves.[18] Both Doty and Johnson write of their experiences in the context of finding meaning and discovering their place within the cosmos. They do so in an attempt to cope with the tragedy which has invaded their lives with the deaths of the ones they loved. It is a way to make life whole again. As they value what they had, they lead themselves and their readers into the more inclusive range of human life itself. This is what spirituality is: living consciously and finding meaning in our relationships. At the very center of who we are as human beings lies our spirituality as we consciously live out our human experience.

Human Experience

To live as human beings is to experience our basic constitution as body-spirit realities. The world is our stage, and living includes the discovery of meaning as well as the enfleshing of that discovery in a relationship with all that is. We are not meant simply to *go through* life. We are to live it, to experience it in the totality of who we are as body-spirit persons. As human beings each of us is concerned with the totality of who and what we are in the world. People, events, choices, sexuality, and nature constantly challenge us to integrate everything in the very persons we are. To be alive is to be and become who one is. It is a process, a journey of fulfillment. That process is not simply finding a career or establishing a family (whether of choice or biological). But from the very beginning, each of us is in the process of becoming fully ourselves. That becoming is the very process which calls us to move beyond the self into community. The realities which are the chosen constitutive values empower us to become more authentically who we are. Authenticity remains the key word: discovering, knowing, and living out our true selves rather than hiding behind a mask.

Living life in view of those values we choose as foundational gradually causes the mask we have created to fall away. From the moment we begin to socialize with other human beings, we begin the process of presenting our selves in the way we think others want us to be. We begin a process of building a mask behind which we hide our real selves from others and often from ourselves as well. As we begin to become conscious of what we have done, we gradually let the mask fall away, though often it is a struggle because we fear rejection if others know who we really are. More and more, however, as we live out of and present the *real* self each of us has come to discover, we see that what is important is authentically being the self even if others reject us. Coming out as a gay man constitutes one of the essential steps in that process of integration and authenticity which is the letting go of the false mask which we created because of the expectations of others.

Seeing and choosing a value around which to build our lives, we empower ourselves to live authentically. This integrating process frees us to leave our mark of humanization in this world. While that discovered and chosen value transcends us, it nonetheless is part of us as enfleshed persons. It opens us to others, to life, and to the world. It is an integral part of our being-in-the-world. It creates for us that unique dynamic of the life which is ours and which constitutionally changes all humanity's experience of the world precisely because everyone and everything is interrelated.

In other words, the choosing of that value and integrating it makes us aware of the fact that we are part of a whole. In fact, we discover that we are so connected with everyone and everything that the whole cannot be what it is and what it is meant to be unless each of us lives out our particular being as authentically as possible. Life calls each of us to live in this mystery of relatedness, and doing so we find ourselves more alive than ever before.

Gay men living out this dynamic claim, affirm, and live authentically every dimension of their personalities, including sexuality. If we are integrating persons, we are neither those who leave aside the physically intimate relations in life, nor are we those who remain *entrapped* in the physical dimension of our existence as if we were nothing but bodies. To deny physicality or spirit (intimacy) keeps us from the wholeness we seek as human beings. Caring, respecting, and loving the other at some level brings us to a real pleasure in making love as well as seeing and affirming our process of integration into fully mature human beings. This is what the conversations and statements I noted at the beginning of this chapter revealed. For we are essentially sensual-spiritual beings, which means we cannot leave either element aside without being but half a person.[19]

This has important ramifications for our relationships with others. Daniel A. Helminiak says that

> someone so integrated would be whole in every one of life's activities and personal encounters, so such sexually and spiritually integrated expressions of love might not be reserved for only one other person. This is not to suggest that someone share sex with everyone he or she meets — nor even with a select number of people — though the latter might indeed happen.[20]

We may or may not be in a completely monogamous relationship. Nonetheless, authentic sexuality moves us constantly into full relationship with the other. Our self-isolation is destroyed to the extent that we do in fact open ourselves out as fully as we can at any given moment to the one with whom we interact in love and concern. Furthermore, this very act of intimate, physical love moves us into a relationship with all that is. We discover our oneness with the whole of reality and seek to enhance the very life of the other, of creation (nature), and even that *power greater than myself*. It is a dynamic of discovery of true mutuality in all our relationships.[21] We discover meaning which includes our sexuality and all elements of our constitutional self. In choosing that meaning-value as the goal in the whole of our lives, we move beyond the self as individualistic and into community.

Finding that value and living it requires a consciousness or awareness of all that surrounds us. The Vietnamese Buddhist monk Thich Nhat Hanh offers ways by which we can develop our consciousness.[22] By paying attention to everyday activities we find treasures which we hardly suspected were present throughout our lives. Our awareness of otherness leads us to finding that value which gives meaning and to affirm it as the raison d'être of one's life. This is the very core of spirituality. This transforms the here-and-now from just a dot in time into an integral part of the becoming of the person each of us is — who we are in time.

Consequently, it is not only possible to have an authentic spirituality which is nonreligious, but spirituality rooted in human experience remains absolutely essential for a healthy, whole human being. With it we see beyond the now, yet it infuses this moment and every moment with growth-producing dynamism. To be human is to become more and more sensitive, more alive, and more self-affirming within the whole community of humanity in which we live. If we live within that context of values which we have chosen, we feel alive and we contribute to the life of the world. Then we are living an authentic spirituality, whether it is theistic, atheistic, or religious. For it comes from within the very structure of our beings as human. It is a structure which calls for an openness to all that surrounds us and contains mystery-producing wonder and appreciation in whatever part of the journey we experience.

Faith

In the human journey to wholeness, we can only trust our own experience of life, the wisdom which we have accrued through trial and error. We seek and find a value which seems consonant with who we are as human beings. Yet, that seeking and finding a value do not depend simply upon our own intuitive powers as if we were totally isolated beings. We seek and discover through our own experience but always cognizant that we are part of a human community which over the centuries has sought that same wisdom through its own process of living life. As gay men we know that that same human community has rarely been welcoming to us. At various times it has tortured us. It has burned us at the stake. It has condemned us to the concentration camps. It has rejected us and effectively removed us from a full participation in society. Yet, we have survived and we have found each other and formed communities made up of other gay men and lesbians as well as straight gay-positive persons. Being authentically who we are has made of us pariahs of society more often than not. Nonetheless, our spirituality remains and even develops not only within this strangely negative context but even because of it.

Only faith in our path enables us to grow and develop.

> Deciding to trust their own *experience, understanding,* and *judgment,* lesbians and gays are in fact engaging their own spiritual capacity.... They affirm the validity of their own selves, and without a road map they launch out in individuality on life's course. Trusting in themselves and in the mixed wisdom of their companions, they live by faith. Only the longings of their heart and soul provide a compass for the journey.[23]

Through a variety of interactions and actualizing of our fundamental value as human beings we can grow and thus challenge the human community in which we live to discover authentic values. If we forge our own paths in spirituality by faith, we do so always in intimate relationship with the members of the human community, foremost with our gay brothers and sisters, but also with others as well. That spirituality is based upon our trust in our own experience and in the often perilously gained insights of others who journey with us. That trust empowers us to say, "This is right for us and contributes to our wholeness as human beings and by that very fact contributes to the wholeness of the world and the human community as such."

There is no absolute certainty. There only remains the affirmation of our choice based upon the conviction that this is how we can be faithful to the reality that we are as gay men. For it is only in being who we are and becoming more fully who we are that we live in and develop community. It is by *faith* in our experience and that of others that we struggle to affirm and live out our values in the face of tremendous opposition from societies which demand absolute conformity to a majority perspective, which is itself unsure of the way to wholeness.

Faith is always a *choice* to trust and be committed. Such a choice involves a struggle. There is the struggle against the *world,* which says that it is foolish. There is the struggle against a self that wants things to be accomplished in another, easier way. There is the struggle against the sometimes crippling fear that one could be wrong. Yet, through it all, the gay man trusts his conviction that this is the only path for him to authenticity and a deeper humanizing life.

This trust and commitment which is faith permeates and enhances our human experience. All that is of faith-life is indeed human life lived in authenticity. This faith does not do away with human life. Rather it colors the believer's life and deepens it. For the believer the enhancement brought about by faith empowers the person to enter the journey toward personal wholeness which involves others and contributes to the becoming of the human community.

A nonreligious spirituality, then, involves human experience, consciousness, interrelatedness, trust, transcendent values, integration and movement into wholeness and authenticity. Sandra M. Schneiders sums it up very well in her description of this humanist spirituality: "In short spirituality refers to the experience of consciously striving to integrate one's life in terms not of isolation and self-absorption but of self-transcendence toward the ultimate value one perceives."[24] This spirituality is necessarily a human experience because it involves consciousness. Seeing and choosing an all-encompassing value (ultimate value), one chooses deliberately to make it truly an enfleshed part of one's life (to integrate one's life). This choice is not simply a one-time act, but is rather a continuous process throughout one's life. In this process, the person moves out of selfishness and self-centeredness into community. This process is not a self-transcendence that denies the authentic self. Rather in transcending the self, one affirms the true self in relationship to others and the world in which one lives. Moreover, one enfleshes the value one has chosen as of ultimate concern for one's existence as a fully human being.

Religious Spirituality

For those who are believers in Jesus Christ, a religious spirituality will necessarily take on the distinctive color of their particular faith stance. After speaking of spirituality in a humanist sense as a quest for value, Michael Downey says,

> This quest takes on a specifically religious dimension when the person's ultimate concern is God, or when the highest ideal is understood as presence to or union with God. It becomes specifically a Christian form of spirituality when it is actualized by the gift of the Holy Spirit which brings about a relationship with God in Jesus Christ and others in the community which bears his name and lives by Christ's Spirit.[25]

What makes this definition distinct is its reference to God manifested in Jesus Christ. The ultimate value which guides and directs the whole life of the person who so chooses it is the Trinitarian God of Christianity. Yet, this does not mean that enfleshment is totally abstracted from any created reality. Far from it. A truly Christian spirituality is a human experience which is religious and which includes a variety of dimensions of life including politics, sexuality, ethics, justice, poverty, consumerism, and ecology.[26] Anything that is human must by its very definition include this whole range of flesh-spirit reality which constitutes human life as such.

As Downey noted, what is important in any spirituality and, therefore, Christian spirituality is the community dimension. Without that, one remains enslaved to a self that imprisons and destroys relationality which is constitutive of human life. Such a lack of relationality makes self-transcendence impossible. For a Christian spirituality, the believing community becomes the locus of the integrating process. More specifically, that community is the church to which those of Christian faith belong and in which they live.[27]

For most contemporary writers on the subject, Christian spirituality has all the same characteristics as that of nonreligious spirituality. Its specificity lies in the discovery and choice of the God manifested in Jesus Christ by the Spirit as one's ultimate value in integrating one's life. This means that the whole of the person's life with all that it contains of attitudes, activities, relationships, concerns, and physicality — including sexuality — is taken into the vision of the loving and compassionate God incarnate in Jesus Christ. It involves then a relationship of mutuality with others, with the world, and with God.

Mutuality with Each Other

To be in a relationship of mutuality with others requires a particular stance of relating with the human community. This stance affirms that all human beings are equal, yet created in such a way that they are not alone in living their lives. Human interaction involves not only a receiving but a giving so that each person and the community find life-enhancing potential within each and every relationship. Sexual and genital interaction produces that same life for the people involved when both affirm their mutuality in making love. Every act of making love, with all its variety of forms, becomes something positive and creative of the human capacity for authentic relation when both express their respect and concern, delight and pleasure at being so intimately one. Such acts of love move both persons into creating a human community founded upon such erotic and, at the same time, altruistic intimate relating. Societies change. Racism lessens. Love prevails. A dream? Perhaps. But these are the possibilities where Love reigns. Such was the essential teaching of that man from Nazareth. Love and the whole of creation are transformed into a reality of wonder and awe. For Love moves the individual out of selfishness and into a community of life.

Mutuality with Creation

Mutuality with the world too is part of spirituality in Christian as well as humanist spirituality. Living this spirituality radically alters the human relationship with nature. In it, the human community so transformed by mutuality sees nature as something not to be dominated and controlled so much as to be nurtured. In that process, the human community itself discovers that it is nurtured as well. We receive from creation, but only in proportion as we give to nature the possibilities for it to fully develop its own potential. All this develops in the harmony which was always meant to exist between humanity and nature itself.[28] We live in constant relationship with our world, which gives us the air we breathe, the food that sustains us, and the shelter we need, as well as the possibility to enjoy the beauty and wonder that surrounds us. In grateful mutuality, we human beings provide nature with protection and the possibility to grow, enhancing thereby our own cycles of life.

Mutuality with God

However, perhaps the most wonder-filled aspect of mutuality in Christian spirituality lies in one's relationship with God in Jesus Christ. An authentic spirituality leads one into a relationship with God with whom each one becomes so united that each gives and receives from the other. Based upon the mystery of the incarnation of the Word of God in Jesus Christ, this mutuality affirms both the goodness of the person's humanity with all its embodiment and a God who so loves all things that God comes to live and speak with us as friends.[29] The God made known in Jesus Christ dares to share our life with us. God loves, suffers, plays, laughs, and rejoices not only with us but in and through us. Furthermore, this God gives us to live the divine life now. All that which constitutes divine being is given us as we give God to live our life as human beings in all our enfleshments. The whole mystical tradition of all faiths has shown the incredible depth of this special relationship. God becomes the lover of the human community and of individuals within that community. God is not only *agapé* but *eros* as well. In this divine-human mutuality, God gives life and love to us, but this same God passionately needs and desires us. The Song of Songs in the Hebraic-Christian tradition is one of the most evidently erotic expressions of the divine-human love in which all human beings live with God by faith as they develop in their spirituality.

In the last analysis, Christian spirituality is pure gift from the Spirit of God to the whole of humanity. It is grace given us by the loving and compassionate God. The discovery of that ultimate value around which and in which we integrate our lives as human beings is offered to us by God in our context, that is, in the circumstances of our lives. Consequently, for the Christian, the discovery of God as *being-for-us* is incarnated and deeply sacramental.

This means that we do not discover this truth like some bolt of lightning which hits us out of the blue. Rather it is found in the events and people which constitute the very life which we live. To make this truth our own, believers respond in that trusting commitment which we call faith. This faith involves Christians in a loving relationship with God in Jesus who lives among us and in a hope which grounds our whole life of relationship with God, the world, and our fellow human beings.

Authentic spirituality, in whatever form it takes, destroys the body-spirit split to engage us in a life which values and enhances bodiliness and interrelationship. As we discover and claim that ultimate value which gives meaning to life, we enter the process of living a spiritual life which is in fact living authentically the self we really are. The authentic self and the value surface as we relate with others. That interaction reveals the value most consonant with the development

of our own authenticity. That ultimate value may be love or compassion or justice or respect or a host of other values around which
and in which human beings can and do construct a way of life which
empowers us and others to truly live in an enfleshed, human way.

A nonreligious spirituality entails the finding of that ultimate value
and enfleshing it in one's own life. It may be agnostic, atheistic, or
theistic without connection with a specific church. Yet it is nonetheless whole and life-creating. That value creates within persons a
movement to an ever-deepening relationship to the mystery which
life is. It may involve them in a whole activist kind of life in which
they find the authentic self. It may involve them in the simplest life of
respectful and compassionate relationship with others and nature —
a relationship which always remains constructive of the other and
nature. It enhances their sexuality and their sexual identity, including their genital expressions, making them truly the embodiment of
their authentic selves. For the gay man, spirituality does not remove
the fact that he loves men. Rather it affirms and empowers him to
make love authentically to those men he loves so passionately.

In a religious spirituality, the believers who are Christians find and
claim as the ultimate value the God made known in Jesus Christ
through the Spirit. They enter an enfleshed life which integrates divine life here and now. Because the life of this God is necessarily one
of absolute love and compassion, in total relatedness with all that
is, the integrating value produces in the believer a life in which the
dynamic of love takes precedence over everything else. Their sexuality too expresses itself in a variety of ways, including genital giving
and receiving, and gradually enhances their relationships with others,
with nature, as well as with God.

Both humanist and religious spiritualities are equally valid. One is
not better than the other except in the sense that it is better for the
one who chooses it. In an existential sense, the gay man who chooses
a humanist spirituality chooses the better way for him. The same is
true for the gay man who chooses religious spirituality. Each one
chooses the path to his full empowerment as a human being relating
to the mystery of life and lives in awe and wonder in that life which
is always embodied.

Chapter 2

To Meet for a Lifetime

What is it to be a lover? To stand alone while seeking to share all that we are with another human being? Every person is born with the desire to bond with another in an intimacy that creates one authentic life for two individuals. The movement of this desire is always toward the other. As we go out of ourselves, the other finds in our movement toward him the challenge to break out of isolation and respond in love with openness to the mystery of life. Our deepest experience is this urge to relate intimately, thus daring to share all that we are both in body and spirit, as the one being we know ourselves to be.

Our earliest experiences as children are those of wanting love and gradually learning to give love to others. At the core of who we are there is a passionate yearning for fulfillment which can only be found in a relationship of mutuality with another human being. This is true for every person, gay or straight. However, in societies filled with homophobia, gay men are told that who we are is not "natural," and consequently, we cannot pursue what constitutes us as persons.

Although gay men have often internalized society's repressive attitudes, in recent years a new reality has entered our lives. Though this reality is overwhelmingly tragic and horrible in itself, it has also laid bare society's superficial perception of us. AIDS opens society to the reality of gay love in new ways. It shows us that gay lovers exist, and our commitment often astounds even the most unbelieving. Medical professionals, families, clergy, and friends attest to the authentic love between gay men who live in this context of HIV/AIDS. We find gay couples struggling to live within all social levels. We are poor, middle class, and wealthy. We are people of color, white people, and Native peoples, brought together in the one struggle to live.

As Hiro struggled with toxoplasmosis and PCP, I met an Afro-American mother whose son, a lawyer, lay dying in a room nearby. Her son's white partner spent all night sleeping on a cot next to his lover, providing the mother a chance to go home and rest. In another room, a man in his late twenties struggled for life as his elderly mother waited alone and hoped that this would not be the time when she would lose him. We met in the halls. We met in the AIDS ward lounge of the hospital. We found in each other the hope that enabled us to provide strength to our lovers, our sons in those rooms. We lived in love.

At the heart of each of these stories is the recognition by gay men that our deepest desire for fulfillment can be found in relationship with another man. We find wholeness in our relationship with the one who sometimes no longer recognizes us as the disease ravages not only his body, but his mind as well. Even amid grief, we remember the miracle of our meeting and loving. Love has been our reason for our being there and remaining there, even as we wonder how we can keep on providing care.

Our stories contain the core of our spirituality. As we have seen, spirituality is not ethereal or otherworldly. It is the all-pervasive thread which makes life dynamic and truly human. It is what enables partners to make life human in the midst of inhuman suffering and social prejudice.

While gay men search for the one to share their lives with in a partnership which enhances both lives, the heterosexist and patriarchal structures of North American society continue to present formidable obstacles. Despite Stonewall and the consequent development of gay movements in North America, gay men have to find their own ways of meeting in a still unfriendly societal structure. The usual patterns of meeting a lifemate are not fully open to them. Teenage dating, dances, and proms remain limited for the most part to male-female couplings.[30] Continued support for the status quo means that gay men have to claim and develop their own stories, their own means of being who they are. Little by little, they have done that, creating a culture within a culture — a place where they might feel safe and find fulfillment as gay men. Yet, the very creation of that culture has its own problems.

Gay culture exists amid and in response to an antagonistic surrounding culture that gay persons constantly imbibe. To combat the pain of recognizing one's alienness, some gay people buy into the myth that all is well. In doing so, we fail to embrace the exile which, as Fortunato tells us, is the only way to depth and fullness of life.[31] In internalizing the fear and the hatred which remain the heart of homophobia, elements of our gay culture can contain negative and self-destructing realities such as drug use, excessive drinking, the inability to trust others, or the reduction of human beings to a penis or a body beautiful.[32] What is remarkable, though, is that despite the odds, gay men do find life and happiness precisely as gay men because they claim their gay identity within a culture which is so hostile. Our stories show that.

These stories need to be told — stories of meeting the one who made an incredible difference in our lives and stories of our discovery of the seropositive status of the one we loved. Here are some of those stories, which situate spirituality in a flesh-and-blood context.

Human Interaction

Meeting someone with whom you ultimately share one life can take place in a variety of circumstances. It can happen by chance or it can be well planned. It can be the result of a determined search for that significant other or just a casual meeting without any thought of having this person become the center of your life.

However it happens, results often come unexpectedly, even when there was a specific plan. Indeed, some find that it is when they have given up hope that they receive that marvelous gift of finding their true selves in relationship to another. While it may all seem rather romantic to an outside observer, the wonder of relationship which develops is something which takes place through the painful clashes and resolutions *as well as* in the shared happy and passionate times. No relationship is immune to suffering. By the very fact of entering a relationship with another human being, we engage ourselves in a dynamic of two different life stories. It is precisely the differences that create the richness of the process of discovery and the ultimate partnership-in-life.

These differences create both the conflicts and the harmonies in which the growth of the two merges into a oneness which does not destroy their individuality but rather enhances it. John of the Cross, a sixteenth-century Spanish mystic, provides a keen insight into the dynamic of all human interrelating. In offering advice to priests and nuns, he said they should not expect that just by being in a monastery, with other people who are seeking to be whole, everything would be fine:

> You should understand that those who are in the monastery are craftsmen placed there by God to mortify you by working and chiseling at you. Some will chisel with words, telling you what you would rather not hear; others by deed, doing against

you what you would rather not endure; others by their temper-
ament, being in their person and in their actions a bother and
annoyance to you.[33]

John is telling us that the very fact of relating to other human beings puts us in situations where we are forced to look at ourselves
honestly. Relationship spurs the development of the authentic self,
which often hides under a mask we create because of what we think
others want us to be. Interrelating destroys the inauthentic self as
human beings consciously engage in seeking out and being with another. This happens in even the most casual of contacts. However,
in a relationship of intimacy and love, it is even more pronounced.
In daring to meet and authentically share life with another we find
not only the other, but we find who we really are and who we are
meant to be in life.

When two people meet and decide to enter a lifelong relationship,
they discover differences. As they seek to harmonize those differences, conflict necessarily arises. That conflict challenges both to take
a long, hard look at who they are and who they truly want to be. It
makes each one reevaluate what is important in life. It chips away
at the masks and gradually allows them to find the inner self which
events, choices, and other people have helped to mask. In a relationship, the microcosm of a couple's world magnifies the mask precisely
because their shared love makes the relationship so intimate, so intense. The relationship brings each to the point of seeing, if he dares,
the falseness he has taken on. And it provides to both the possibility
of letting that mask go and affirming the authentic self each one is.

Relationship, them, is the process of discovery and growth. The
habits of the other sometimes grate. The excitement of making love
often wanes with time. When these things happen, each one needs
to take a closer look — perhaps not so much at the other as at oneself. "What is it that makes me react this way?" "Why am I angry?"
"What do I really want in life, in this relationship?" At first, one
places the blame on the other. "It's his fault. He doesn't really listen
to me." "I keep telling him not to do this, but he continues, almost
as if to goad me on." Yet, what is needed is to listen to the inner self
as it tries to speak at these times. The other is a gift to me to discover
who I am — and this is a mutual affair. I too am a gift to the other:
to enable him to let go of the mask and find his real self. Relationships are discoveries and life to those who dare to put themselves
into them.

Dating

Jack and Jerry

Jack met his partner Jerry at an AA meeting. "I was sitting in an AA meeting listening to a speaker talk about his life and recovery. And he looked at me and I looked at him. He says now that he laid the look on me and I didn't have a chance. . . . I had gone not expecting to meet anyone. . . . I didn't expect to find a partner there that I would be spending the rest of my life with. It was a year before we decided to be partners. We dated. It was almost a classical dating thing." During that year, they would call each other, go out for dinners or a movie. For many in the gay culture, this was strange. "When I tell people in the gay world we dated for a year, they look at me as if to say, 'What do you mean you dated? You mean you just didn't move in together?' " Jack and Jerry decided that they wanted to have a monogamous relationship rather than an open one. While Jerry had never been in a long-term relationship, Jack had. Four years before they met, Jack and his former lover had broken up after a six-year relationship. The differences in Jack's and Jerry's experiences did not stop them from establishing their life together. Rather they were the foundation for it. "And so the relationship evolved from that."

"We were happy at first and still are. I was traveling a lot with my work, and so our relationship slowly melded together. We moved in together after a year, but I was traveling every week and was home on the weekends. So it was like we were still dating. Then my job changed and we were together more of the time. About a year into our relationship we decided we wanted to move." They found a place where they thought it would be great to live, though it was expensive. To have the money they would need they decided they would have to open a business.

After moving and getting settled, Jerry "told me he felt he needed to be tested for HIV. He said he would just feel better. Jerry got tested, and he tested positive. . . . It's impacted our relationship a lot as I guess you know it would." Their private physician did the test, and shortly afterward, while they were at their store, Jerry got a call from him. The doctor gave him the results over the phone. "It really devastated him, and he told me right then and there."

At that point, Jack did not know what his own status was. "At first, I thought, 'It's not true. There must have been some mistake.' . . . I felt unbelievably sad for a while and yet I thought I had to be strong for him. Now when he told me, I didn't know I was negative. I thought for sure that if he was positive I would be too. My biggest concern was for Jerry because he knew without a shadow of a doubt that he was positive. I didn't know about my own diagnosis. I wanted to help him get through the trouble he was feeling. I prayed. And we just sat down together and talked to each other. It was a life-changing moment. We talked and he was feeling so many emotions. I felt I had to be strong. (I don't know if I really was or not) and I tried to be. I remember clearly asking God to put the words in my mouth so that I would say the right thing. But now it's almost like this is a way we've been drawn together as we wouldn't have been before. We really bonded in our relationship in ways I never imagined could happen."[34]

Jerry's diagnosis as seropositive engaged both Jack and Jerry in a new way of being a couple. The diagnosis was a challenge for both, though evidently in different ways. It forced them to see each other and their life together with new eyes. Through the communication of their hopes, their fears, and the reality they were now called to live, the love and sharing of their lives took on new dimensions. They both found a new life with this intrusion of HIV.

Jason and Karl

Another couple, Jason and Karl, met in a singing class. Jason had noticed Karl and decided that he wanted to get to know him. Although Jason made several attempts to break the ice, Karl showed no interest. Jason figured that there was no hope for any kind of relationship. After a couple of years a common friend arranged a blind date for Jason. As Jason noted, "So the day of our date came, and instead of going out and buying an outfit and doing everything that I normally do, I didn't do anything. I took a nap before I went. And then I got up. I was running late, so I didn't even take a shower." While walking to the Lesbian-Gay Center for the rendezvous, Jason spied a man with red hair, a feature which he had never found attractive. He thought to himself, "Who is that Queen?" Then getting closer, he realized that this was his date. It was Karl! Immediately he thought, "Oh, God! I'm going to go back. I'm tired anyway. I'm not really up for this." But then he caught himself and thought, "No, Jason. You're trying to do things differently, remember?"

Jason and Karl met and talked about what they would do. Though Karl did not seem too enthused by the plan, they decided to go see the film *Longtime Companion*. However, arriving at the theater, they found that it was sold out. So instead, they went for dinner, during which Jason's whole tone changed. "I started talking.... There was like this softness that came over me and I couldn't shut up.... I just found myself really taken with him." Then, just before the dinner ended, Jason realized that he would have to tell Karl that he was HIV positive. Walking to the subway, he finally found the courage to speak: "Karl, I want you to know that I had a really wonderful time.... But there is something I need to tell you." Feeling awkward, he said, "I just want you to know that I'm HIV positive." Karl looked directly at him, saying, "Is that it?" Jason responded, saying, "Yes. You can go now. I'll understand if you want to leave. It's Okay. Don't worry about me." But Karl answered, "That's nothing, because I have AIDS." There were some Kaposi Sarcoma lesions on Karl's face, but Jason, who was not very familiar with the progression of the disease at the time, had simply thought that he had a bad complexion. They spent the night together making love, and this was the beginning of a relationship which was to last until Karl's death, two years later.

Jason had decided right after testing seropositive to become more open to the opportunities that the present offered. Meeting Karl became a chance for him to put his decision into effect. Letting go of old habits, he entered into a relationship which provided him with something for which he had longed. Often we meet people who change our lives in unexpected moments or ways. As both of the preceding stories illustrate, being open to these moments can enable us to find meaning which we had never expected before. Opening to whatever the present moment offers is a key element in any spirituality. Spirituality begins with the breaking down of self-isolation and the opening up of a world which previously had escaped our awareness.

In the Bars

Jake and Ricky

Jake and Ricky met in a leather bar one night. "We had sort of a whirlwind relationship," Jake recounts, "which most of mine are. I think after three months I moved in with him. We were together for about a year, and then he was diagnosed with thrush." Ricky told Jake that he was positive and his T-cell count was very low. "I can't really remember that much. My most vivid recollection of that period was he had thrush. He had a fungus on his tongue. I didn't want to kiss him, and he was upset and felt like I was treating him like a leper. He was very sensitive about being shut out. I think it was mostly because he looked so awful — not because I was afraid of catching AIDS. We had always had safe sex, but we had kissed and had anal sex without a condom but not to ejaculation. So that was the first issue that came up." Jake spoke about how he handled the whole situation at that time: "The way I normally handle my feelings . . . is to not talk about them and pretend they'll go away. But Ricky was much more pushy about that and made me talk about it."

Bars are among the few places where gay men can meet in a relatively secure atmosphere. As we shall see in this section, many partners met there and their relationship developed from that initial encounter. This was the case for Jake and Ricky. Jake's approach to feelings had been to avoid thinking about them and certainly not to talk about them to anyone, even a partner. Yet, Ricky's more communicative attitude changed that and forced Jake to deal with those feelings and express them. This communication was fundamental to their relationship. As it happened, they each discovered new aspects of themselves and the other which formed the beginning of a deeper spirituality.

Stan and Mario

A variety of things, including physical characteristics, can attract people to one another. This was the case for Stan. "We went to a bar and there he was. When I went up and started talking to him I thought he had such an extraordinarily beautiful face. I thought that if his personality was anywhere near the beauty of his face, we would certainly get along very well. Which we did. He was absolutely friendly and wonderful. We spent four days together and went to a swimming pool party at friends of mine and then a dinner party." At the time Stan had been staying with a friend; he was on his way to visit his family and then planned to take a short holiday in another city. His friend said to him, "You have to leave because if you don't you'll never take your trip." Though he desperately wanted to stay with Mario, Stan finally decided he should continue the trip as planned.

After he returned Stan wanted to get back in touch with Mario. "I came back and called him. We spent another four days together, and then I said I wanted to spend the rest of my life with him. He said, 'Well, I will have to come and see what I am getting into — where you live, how we would live and do things, and how I'd feel there.'"

They lived in different cities quite distant from each other. Mario flew up to Stan's place to spend the weekend. Shortly after his return home, Mario called Stan telling him to come and get him. This was the beginning of a relationship which lasted for fifteen years until Mario died.

They started a rather successful business together, renovating Victorian houses, but then several of Stan's friends started getting sick.[35] Stan experienced the devastation that AIDS was wreaking on his community. With the pressure of their work and so many of their friends becoming ill, they decided they needed to get away. Both Stan and Mario set about planning a break, which they hoped would give them the relaxation they needed. The night before they were to leave for the trip, Mario began coughing and had a fever and chills. However, despite Stan's suggestions that they cancel the trip, Mario insisted they go anyway. The second day of the trip he got worse, and so they decided to return home, and Stan checked Mario in to the Veterans Hospital. Two hours later the doctor informed Stan that Mario had pneumocystis pneumonia. This was in 1990. Stan says, "I almost knew what they were going to tell me, and, having been through so much with my ex-lover, I knew the symptoms. On the way to the hospital, I prayed it wouldn't be that. But if it was that, I knew we had to deal with it and enjoy every moment because I knew our time would be limited. I was tough as nails. I never cried before. I never cried for twenty-five years about anything until Mario died, and now I can't stop crying. . . . Even when my other friends died, I never cried. I was just awfully sad. Now I'm crying for everybody. This was the most crucial person in my life, so I had to face the greatest loss I've ever known. I'm HIV positive myself, but it doesn't particularly scare me. I'm at peace with whatever will happen. I've had a good life."

At the time of the interview, it had been but a short time since Mario's death. The love which Stan and Mario had for each other came through very clearly in Stan's reminiscing about their life together. It had been an immediate and mutual attraction despite Mario's wanting to know more about Stan's situation and how they would make a living.

Chris and Phil

Chris and Phil had also met in a bar in 1983, but Chris was not interested in getting into a relationship as he had never been in one before. He was quite happy the way he was. However, he did find

Phil rather intriguing. So they dated for a long time before getting an apartment together. Chris says, "I was spending most of my time at his place, which was a change for me. In previous relationships they always came to my place." Phil was diagnosed about four years after they had met. Chris had been away on a business trip, and he knew that Phil would be getting his test results. Upon his return Phil told him that he was positive. "I felt, in a way, as devastated as I did with the death of my parents or my brother. It seemed like a death sentence. We had been in the process of house hunting, and we put that on the back burner."

Chris says, "Unfortunately, although I have been involved in adult children of alcoholics, I really stuffed the feelings and went on from there. It was a very difficult time. It was a couple of months before Phil and I came together again sexually." Even before the diagnosis, but only after two and a half years into their relationship, they practiced safe sex. Phil went for a physical and had his T-cells counted, and they were high. The HIV antibody test came back negative for Chris. He felt devastated that it was negative. This was something he wasn't going to share with Phil.

Their first couple of years together were rather tumultuous. They went to counseling for couples, but "it wasn't working. It was too painful for him and I didn't want to put him through it. So I decided I would make the compromises necessary to make the relationship work. But I was very uncertain about that." After a time, Chris had decided that the relationship was over and was going to tell Phil after a visit from Phil's family. However, something unexpected happened during that visit, and it changed everything. "Seeing him with his family was just wonderful. I had no questions about the relationship from that point on."

Chris had studied Christian Science. "I felt it would give me the basis I would need to be there for him and to get in touch with my spiritual self so that I would have the strength to get through what lay ahead." Yet, Phil's illness and particularly his death "continues to be the most devastating experience I've ever had. I found it much more difficult than I thought it would be.... My life will never be the same. I'm a completely different person than I was because of my relationship with Phil and because of other circumstances. I'm in recovery, but I don't think I'll ever recover."

While some relationships develop clearly and easily, Chris and Phil's followed a different path. It took them through some difficult times as they tried to break through the obstacles that presented themselves. A seemingly ordinary visit from Phil's family became the breakthrough Chris needed to complete the journey in relationship. Through it all there was a love and concern which, even if he was not conscious of it at the time, enabled them to break through and grow. For Chris relationship proved to be about becoming "a completely different person." His mask fell away, and he found a new life in this relationship.

Dennis and Hal

Though Dennis had first met Hal in a bar, he would find that their relationship came about through an unusual set of circumstances. One of Hal's roommates invited Dennis to a birthday party at their place. Presuming that Hal was this roommate's date, Dennis went to the party only to discover that the guy had four dates and was moving around, sitting with them all at different times. Upset by this turn of events, Dennis decided to leave and went out to a bar. Hal ended up there too with two of his roommates. They talked, and "I invited them back to my place and that was the way we [Hal and he] started."

They moved into their own place in 1985, but Hal's former lover caused some problems. He would call to annoy them for a long time. Then, after six weeks' silence, he called again. After the call, Dennis saw that something was troubling Hal. "He was really quiet and didn't say much, and I knew something was bothering him, but I didn't know what. Finally, I came out and asked him, 'What's on your mind? Is it that phone call?' He said it was the phone call he had received. He said he didn't know what to think of it." Dennis said that Hal's former lover had called to say that he had tested HIV positive and that he had been HIV positive and never told Hal. "He told Hal it might be a good idea to be tested and that I be tested as well. So that was the way we learned. We made an appointment right away. Hal went for his test and his test came back positive. My test came back negative but the doctor told me that because of my sexual practices I should go back in a year."

But Dennis had to deal with Hal's diagnosis. "I was really scared about it. I was nervous about it. I had heard about AIDS in the eighties and had tried to educate myself about it. At that point, people didn't live long, and I was nervous about that. I really loved Hal and felt really close to him. I told him I would still love him, and that was it." They talked with each other about this and many other things in their deepening relationship. Knowing that time could be at a premium now, they spent as much time together as they could. In the process of their talking, they made a very serious decision, one which would affect them both as time went on. "We decided we were not going to disclose this to anyone else, that we were going to keep it between ourselves, and that is what we did. We didn't disclose it to our family or to our friends. We educated ourselves as much as we could to protect my cousin who was living with us, so we wouldn't transmit it accidentally."

Steve and Sean

"My lover was Sean. I knew about him before I met him. I went to a bar and was told he was at another bar. So I went there. I wanted to check this out. The stories I had heard about him were kind of intriguing. So I went over to the bar, and he picked me up."

"At the time he didn't really believe in relationships. He had just come out of the closet even though he was with a girl for about five years. He broke up with her and came out, so to speak. He started going to the bars, and that's how I met him. To me, I thought it was going to be another one-night thing. I called him a couple of days later, and he didn't sound too interested. So, I said, 'Okay. Well, I'll let you go.' Then he said, 'No. No.' So we talked some more."

"He was just getting into the party mode and all that, which I was already into. That's how we started the relationship. I said I wanted an open sort of relationship." There was no question at this time of being in a monogamous relationship. Steve and Sean ended up moving in together.

As regards the diagnosis, "He found out on his birthday. We had plans for the weekend, and he kept it in and didn't want to tell me right away. That Sunday he was sitting on the couch, and I went to hold his hand and it was really cold. I said, 'Oh, my God, you feel like a corpse.' He just sort of laughed and then he said, 'Well, I have something to tell you.' He told me his last test came back positive. He went for a test because he was getting sick all the time. He had had a check-up a couple of weeks before and the doctor had said he didn't need an HIV test because he had had one two years before. But he did anyway and it came back positive this time....The part I remember most was when he told me. I kind of backed away from him. I guess it was a natural fear or something. I thought about it after, and he started to cry saying, 'You don't have to stay if you don't want to.' I just told him that as long as we we're together, we'll be Okay."

Steve's own reaction was to see a doctor. "I wanted to know for myself too. It was kind of hard, but the doctor wasn't that surprised. I hadn't seen a doctor in a long time. I started getting my health on track. I wanted to cut down on the partying. . . . Well, I've learned so much about it now. It's pretty well an educational process. I feel I have a lot more knowledge about it now, and it's not as scary."

What seems to be just a casual encounter can actually turn out to be something much more permanent. This was the case with Steve and Sean. Even though he'd entered into the relationship, Steve still was not interested in any kind of purely monogamous arrangement. He wanted to be able to see other guys and have sex with them if he so desired. Yet, for them both, the relationship developed into something radically different as they grew to be more and more committed to each other despite the entry of HIV into their relationship. Sean had offered Steve the chance to leave right after he told him of his diagnosis. However, Steve's response indicated to both that this relationship was not to be let go of that easily. Steve's saying that they would be fine together was his commitment to their life together. It was the realization for Steve that this was indeed something he wanted, something essential for his own life as well as Sean's.

Darin and Emile

After a while, it is not unusual for gay men to think that they will never find "Mr. Right." They want to find the perfect man, but it never seems to happen. They try and try, but each time they fail to find that relationship for which they long. But then, having given up hope, there he is. Darin found this to be the case the night he met Emile in a bar.

"I had reached a point in thinking that I would always be single, but things sort of happened. The night I got home . . . I had a good feeling about him. I gave it six weeks. I thought it was just infatuation and that it would last six weeks. Emile was excited as each week passed. Then when the sixth week came, it was like a carnival. It was sort of like now we were partners or lovers. I sort of said no, but not having been in a relationship I had nothing to go on. I had doubts about the scary business of getting into a relationship. . . . By nine months into the relationship, I knew I loved him and that he loved me. . . . I allowed him to love me, to let myself be loved, to see that I was worth loving. It took a long time for me."

"Basically, the relationship itself was very happily monogamous. He was a flight attendant. Flight attendants are always busy, and you always think they are given opportunities to have sex. For me, there was no question about trust. We were together about six years. Actually the relationship went very quickly. Last week when I went through all the letters and stuff — I hadn't done that since he died — I found a note he had written seventeen days after we met saying how much he loved me."

During their relationship, Emile decided he wanted to get tested to have the test behind him. "I think Emile had slept with a total of five men in his life. I was sort of the slut of the family, and I didn't want to know. I'm sort of a hypochondriac in some ways, and I can worry myself to death — every sneeze, every cough." So Darin told him to go ahead and get tested by himself. They had gotten together in October 1988, and Emile was tested in June 1989. The day came for getting the results, but Darin did not hear from him. Darin called, but there was no answer. "Then I knew it was bad news. Finally, he called later and in a little voice said that he was positive and that he could understand my wanting to end the relationship and not wanting to live through it. I can't recall if I'd thought about it, but I knew there was no question that he was still going to be in my life. We basically just lived our lives to the fullest.... We had a good life together."

Darin found that though he could be pessimistic about a lot of things, he was optimistic that they would have a long time together or that there would be a cure. Other than talking with his cousin about it, he didn't see any counselors or support groups. "I just tried to be there for him and hoped he'd feel that nothing had changed."

Each person finds his own way to deal with a relationship and a diagnosis. Some people might see Darin as living in denial. Yet, while optimistic, he knew things were still serious. Love and hope carried Darin and Emile along. Their love was deep enough for them to remain with each other. Darin valued Emile and what they had come to create together — this one life. Emile, like Sean, had a love so deep that he was willing to offer Darin the chance to leave once he knew Emile's seropositive status. Certainly, both Emile and Sean did not want their lovers to leave them, but they were willing to take the chance and offer them the possibility. Both were not disappointed.

Sloan and Keith

When I interviewed Sloan and Keith they were both in relatively good health. Both were HIV positive, and I interviewed them separately. They had known each other for over a year before they decided to get together in a relationship. When they met, both were in problematic relationships. Sloan's partner wanted an open relationship. Keith met Sloan when his partner had left him for a while. "We had sex that night and slowly over the weeks and weekends we'd make time to see each other. That friendship grew and went beyond what we call fuck buddies." Sloan had broken up with his lover, and Keith was leaving his by this time. Sloan was already considering moving to another state to be with a guy he was seeing. When he told Keith about moving, Keith said, "What gives? We've got to talk." Then Sloan said, "You mean if I would have asked you to be my lover you would have said yes?" And Sloan responded, "Yes." They talked for hours and decided that this was what they wanted. Later they moved into Sloan's apartment, and then to a house they rented before finally purchasing a home.

Keith had told Sloan he was seropositive. Later when Sloan was tested and found out he was positive as well, Keith wasn't shocked. He had already been on AZT for five years. Sloan found it unnerving, but "it didn't make a difference either. We had been surrounded by so much, and particularly the bar crowd we had hung out with was really hit, really hard. But that was not a reason not to go ahead with the relationship. . . . We talked it through. We talked every step of the way."

Sloan noted something else. "There are so many dynamics in the gay culture that I know. There are so many things set up. To be a real member of the society you have to be able to have sex forty different ways. You have to be able to do this and that. I want to be more responsible and accountable. I understand how you get pulled into different things at different times just in trying to feel good about who you are. . . . I think we have to be prophetically critical in a positive way about our community. If we can change the dynamics of our communities, people wouldn't get stuck in these kinds of things."

As regards his feelings about being positive, Sloan said, "I'm more scared. What the blood tests say and what we experience in our bodies are very different. I know we need those blood tests to know how to take care of ourselves. But they have sort of a debilitating effect psychologically. They should come out and say just being HIV doesn't mean you are going to get full-blown AIDS. Full-blown AIDS doesn't mean you are going to die. So there's optimism and some denial going on. I think there's some support to the idea that being

HIV positive is not a death sentence, but the numbers say other-wise. You feel that you're in good health, but there are the reminders from the blood work. So that scares me. I don't want him to get sick. I feel badly when he even gets a headache. I don't want him to go. Part of the feeling of insecurity is that I fear I won't be a strong enough caregiver if he becomes dependent. We have worked on such a nice mix, over six or seven years, of deepening independence and interdependence. Neither one of us want to be dependent on the other."

What started off as a purely sexual attachment turned into a relationship with strong foundations for Sloan and Keith. Both found in each other what they had been looking for in other relationships. It was a gradual process of discovering in the other the key that made their lives fuller. Their seropositive status proved not to be an obstacle, despite the fact that it can be frightening at times.

Religious Setting

Ken and Lewis

If some people meet at bars or cruising places, it is not surprising that others meet in religious settings. Without trying to create a stereotyp-ical portrait, we can say it is not unusual to find gay men involved in churches or even seminaries. For one reason or another, many gay men find religion helpful, at least at some stage of their lives. The values they discover in organized religion find a home within their own yearnings. (Of course, here I am talking about positive values which are at the heart of authentic religion — in this case, Christian religion.) Many want to be able to offer these values to others. So they become active in churches and often decide to enter seminaries. This was the case with Ken and Lewis

"We met at the seminary. Lewis was going to have lunch with the admissions director and was touring campus as a prospective stu-dent. Something came up at the last minute. The admissions director knew I had a background in finance, and so she asked me to stand in until she got there. We've been together ever since."[36] As they spoke, Lewis told Ken that he was HIV positive.

Lewis had discovered his seropositive status through his doctor and, in their discussions, determined that he had been infected about a year or so before he met Ken. When Lewis told Ken about it, Ken remembers that he was somewhat surprised. "I was a little taken aback but not much. Being new in seminary and not wanting to go against my liberal credentials, my first thought was that the noble, proper, and ethical thing to do was to say, 'That's not a problem. We don't discriminate against people with HIV.' What that meant for me as an individual, I don't know. I had not thought it through and did not care to at the time....I don't remember making a decision: 'Okay. Can I stay with him or not?' As we grew in getting to know one another, it was no longer a question."

Ken had a tendency to put up a brave front in the face of difficulties, and that is what he did. It was Lewis's attitude that Ken found most helpful. Lewis talked about the situation, explaining what different things meant, what could happen. Ken listened intently. "By listening to that I came to see that this was a serious thing but it shouldn't stand between us."

Greg and Al

Four months after being ordained a Jesuit priest, Greg met Al, who belonged to the same Roman Catholic community. Greg went to a dinner at Al's house, and they got along very well that evening. Greg remembers, "There was this kind of electricity there, and when dinner was over we did the dishes and just continued to talk. Interest was being communicated and then he invited me to a party to be held the next week by the community. I went to the party....I had always wanted to be a priest and I was very happy,...and then I fell in love. I didn't expect that to happen."

An authentic intimacy developed. Greg says, "There was a magical spark there, and it was growing. It took me the next year and a half to decide to leave the community. I had always felt called to be a priest, but after a year Al felt he wasn't cut out to be a priest and wanted to work in ministry or social work, which was his training." However, Al was concerned lest his own decision would drag Greg away from the priesthood. They decided together to go through a discernment process to discover what would be the best path for them. During that time they became involved with Dignity, helping to set up a Marriage Encounter program for gay couples. "I remember working on this planning for Marriage Encounter and coming out one Sunday. I told Al I had completed my discernment and wanted to leave the Jesuits. He looked at me and said, 'Let's think for a few minutes.' Fifteen minutes later he said, 'Can we name the dog after my father?' We decided to move in together in November 1977. We exchanged rings quietly."

They wanted to avoid making a fuss over their decision, which might create problems in the community. However, in February 1978 a friend held a shower for them. At that party, some friends of theirs who were in the community attended and afterward called other people in the community to tell them about it. Within a month it was widely known that Greg and Al were together. Things turned out much differently from they had thought or planned. Some members of the community who had been their friends distanced themselves for fear they would be considered gay. Despite the turn of events, Greg and Al continued their new lifestyle, keeping the model of their community and applying it to their relationship. They also kept up a ministry which they felt was deeply important to their relationship — their Dignity involvement.

After having lived together for some time, they decided to be tested for HIV. They wanted to be tested and get the results together, but the system at the time did not allow that. Greg notes, "They wouldn't respect us as a couple. So we had to have it done individually. I was scheduled at 9:30 and he at 10:00. I went and got my results — no problem — and then I went home, about a five-minute drive. He didn't get back for an hour, and so I knew that he was positive. We cried together. It was very traumatic."

"I tried to be very strong for him and at the same time I tried to be as optimistic as possible. Al was not a fighter, and I am a fighter. I was trying to fight for him." Though Greg wanted to contract HIV himself, Al was adamant about not passing the virus on to him. "He knew that I wanted to share his fate. There was a lot of guilt there. When you reach a certain intimacy with a person you don't have to speak the words and thoughts. You know what each is feeling. There's a oneness there. But the feeling of separation was beginning in our lovemaking because we were starting to go on very divergent paths."

Their feelings came out when they spoke with each other. Greg tried to speak of AIDS as a managed illness and how research could offer hope. Yet, deep down they both knew that such a hope at that time was ill founded. Nothing would happen quickly enough to stop the progression of the disease. Their continuing talks started the grieving process for both of them. Greg says, "Dealing with this on a day-to-day basis was very difficult and painful. Instead of denying his status we talked about it. We prayed about it." Greg and Al had met within their religious community, and a communal commitment became the basis for their own life together as a couple. Their love developed to such an extent that they wanted to share everything. Greg even wanted to share being seropositive, not unusual for gay couples when one is negative and the other positive.

Tom and Tim

One Sunday Tom was listening to a young man preach at an MCC service in the city where he had recently decided to live. He had just come out of a nine-year relationship. Though Tom had always wanted to form a relationship with someone closer to his own age, he was struck by this handsome young man. After the service, he started asking others who he was. It was during these discussions that he found out that Tim had a lover. So he tried to forget about anything happening between them. Nonetheless, Tom said, "I started going to church twice on Sunday, trying to see him. The next time I heard him talk he preached about his lover walking out on him, and in the social hour after I introduced myself. I said I'd like to wake up next to him some morning." However, Tim felt that because he was a clerical student it would not be ethical for him to date someone from the church. Tom suggested they get together for dinner sometime and gave Tim his phone number. The very next day, Tim called. That was the beginning of their relationship.

After they had come to know each other, Tom found in Tim what he had been looking for all his life — someone who really cared for him. In his previous relationships and even in his own family, he had not found this. His father had rejected him. As a result, Tom developed a need to care for others in need, perhaps hoping unconsciously that he would find support for himself too. Yet, Tom felt he never had discovered that care and concern until now, with Tim. He fell in love.

Tim knew that he was HIV positive and informed Tom about it. Knowing this made Tom feel that they could never live together. After Tim's first bout with an AIDS-related illness, they talked about death. "I was having trouble with the thought of making love with someone knowing he would end up dying on me and I'd be left alone. It was always on my mind. . . . But we spent more time together, and after six months it was time to move together or split up." They moved in together, but the difficulties remained for Tom: "It's hard to this day to make love to someone who's going to be gone."

At the time of the interview, Tom was seeing a psychiatrist every two weeks, and that particular week they were to speak about Tim's death and how Tom would handle the situation. Tim had made such a difference in Tom's life that he had begun to reestablish self-esteem and in fact, as he said, had "re-created" himself. Tim was a real strength for Tom. "I think probably accepting that he loved me no matter what made me relax. I didn't feel I had to work over-board to prove to him that I was there for him. I became a little more relaxed."

Their relationship had grown over the past six months, but it was not "picture perfect," as Tom would say. There were times of anger and getting very upset. Tom found that he would "have to get out maybe three or four times a day." Yet, the concern he received from Tim enabled him to move through it all, even with the anger.

Duncan and Cliff

Duncan was an Anglican priest who had met Cliff at an Appalachian mountain clogging class. Duncan saw him the first night and found him rather attractive, but Cliff seemed to have no real interest in him despite the fact that they had exchanged phone numbers. After three or four weeks of class, Cliff did not return. Then, about a year later, they met again on Gay Pride Weekend. Hoping they might get together sometime, Duncan said, "Well, it sounds like maybe we should get together for that lunch we've been talking about." Cliff said that he would call after he had cleared up some things in his life. With that, Duncan felt it would not happen. Some time later, he got a call at work and it was Cliff. They arranged to meet at a Gay Rodeo. Their meeting seemed a bit better, but it would be a while before anything more took place.

One day, as Duncan helped a friend paint his house, Cliff showed up and offered to take him out to brunch. Off they went to a fine restaurant in a nearby town where Cliff "wined and dined" him. Taking him back, Cliff said, "You're going to stay overnight." After that, Duncan said, "Well, then I started staying one night a week, then it was two nights a week. By Christmas it was pretty much all the time."

Though Cliff was "formally" diagnosed in 1987, some three or four years before this, he had switched from a couple of doctors to one who was involved very early on in AIDS work. Duncan thought this strange and says, "I think he knew before that. I think it had come up with his other doctors."

"I had actually been tested and come up positive," Duncan said, "and I told him about me. And he said, 'Oh. You can't be.' And went on and on about it. I said, 'Well, I am.' So there was no reason for him not to tell me that he was also positive. But he didn't tell me for months. It was very strange. It was a very strained and strange time. Cliff was a very, very private person." After Cliff told him that he was positive too, Duncan says, "I was very angry. I blew up at him. We got into counseling. We were in counseling for many years, mainly because I felt like I didn't trust everything completely that came from him." Duncan tried to handle his feelings with drinking, while trying to understand what was going on. He got angry at times, but "I had a number of friends who were of support to me, who helped me to stabilize at that point. Friends from the church in particular. And not necessarily gay. Some gay, but mostly heterosexual." Underneath it all though, was Duncan's love for Cliff, which made it possible for him to care for Cliff until his death.

– ◆ –

Within every human person there is deep longing for fulfillment — a fulfillment which only relationships render possible. That openness to the other is the very heartbeat of humanity. We all live our lives permeated by desire for the other. In recognizing this desire we see that one is meant to be for the other. It is in the mystery of the other that we discover our real selves and the real meaning of life.

The gay men in this book have shown how they have dared to seek human fulfillment in love for another man. Their desire for wholeness, found within a life of love with another man, has not been compromised by society's attempts to remove it. It cannot be denied precisely because that desire is so fundamental to being human. Moreover, this openness to the other and thus to mystery is the basis of any spirituality, whether nonreligious or religious. In our desire for the other, we also discover who we are in relationship to the wider universe. None of us is alone. Rather, we find meaning and wholeness in interrelationship, and especially with that significant other with whom we form one life.

Like all human beings, gay men meet that other in a variety of ways. Some have met in bars, some at parties. Some have met through friends, in religious settings. What is important is that they met each other and were able to form loving relationships which would see them through extremely trying times. Most discovered the other when they least expected it. This fact often provides the assurance that the relationship is real and not simply created by a desire.

Some might call the meeting of that special other a mere chance or coincidence. Others might call it God's gift, or fate. Whatever we call it, what cannot be denied is the special reality that meeting precipitates in the lives of the men who came to love and find life in each other. This love and their life together become the foundation for their strength in the crises of their lives.

Chapter 3

Crisis: Risk and Opportunity

When AIDS enters into a relationship, endless unexpected difficulties can occur. Some of these are relatively minor, but others are major ones which create a context of crisis in the relationship. The characters which make up the word "crisis" in Chinese and Japanese provide us with an important insight into a crisis situation: one character means "danger" and the other "opportunity." A crisis can be and often is destructive. However, we must acknowledge at the same time that within the very "crisis" one can find an opportunity for a constructive outcome. Partners of persons living with HIV/AIDS find that situations of difficulty for the one they love provide them with the chance to discover aspects of themselves they had not known before. These characteristics not only enable them to survive very trying situations, but also help their partners to cope with what seems to be destroying their hope.

Whether the partner knew about the seropositivity of his lover before the relationship began or found out afterward, the discovery brings disruption to their life together. When the virus becomes invasive, it can create situations which seem to be more than the caregiving partner can handle, to say nothing of the infected person. Some partners are not able to manage, and simply leave before the illness takes its full toll. On the other hand, there are those who find the inner strength and external support to remain despite the desperateness of the situation. They are determined to live those experiences no matter how physically or emotionally painful they are.

The reactions vary because of the life experiences of the caregivers. An experience of their past may be what enables them to continue despite a seemingly hopeless prognosis. Or perhaps their whole previous life process makes them able to face the challenge that HIV/AIDS brings into a relationship. Their religious background may play a role. How they have previously interacted with family and friends often becomes a determining factor as they try to provide their lovers with support. We can say the same thing for their education and social backgrounds. Each person is an individual with a particular story which becomes the "stuff" of his reaction and action on behalf of his infected lover . We see this in the narratives of partners whose stories are told here.

Day-to-Day Difficulties

Emotional and Physical Stress

The major difficulty which Stan had to face each day centered on seeing Mario become more and more ill, with only the occasional respite. Seeing Mario lose so much weight one week and then regain some of it a few weeks later meant Stan had to adapt to a variety of situations.[37] As Mario was intimately involved in this struggle, Stan, who watched every new mood, every lost pound, struggled to keep himself sane and healthy so he could be there when Mario needed him. One day Stan would find himself filled with dread as the disease seemed to overwhelm them both. The next, he would find hope.

Finally, Stan and Mario saw that things had to change. "After a second bout of pneumocystis we decided that he couldn't work any longer. We decided he was going to be a housewife and work in the garden and make little dinners for friends and just enjoy himself. And if he wanted to travel he could go. But he didn't care to travel unless I went with him." Things became even more complicated when Mario developed the purplish lesions of Kaposi Sarcoma. Following medical advice, Mario began receiving radiation in the hopes of removing the lesions.

The radiation treatments left Mario nauseous and unable to eat or do much else. Furthermore, Mario was very conscious of his appearance. With the lesions appearing, he was devastated. Stan had to adapt to Mario's emotional pain. After the appearance of KS, they decided to rent a cabin in a resort area. One day while they were there, Stan recounts, "He was sitting on the deck at the front of the cabin. He was just skin and bones. I found him crying because he was afraid the neighbors would see how thin he was without his shirt on." To see him in such emotional pain affected Stan deeply. Their love made them so close that in many ways they were one person in two bodies. Their spirits mingled and shared the pain through their love for each other. Such feelings are reminiscent of what Augustine of Hippo said about his relationship with his friend who had died when both were teenagers: "I marveled more that I, his second self, could live when he was dead. Well has someone said of his friend that he is half of his soul. For I thought that my soul and his soul were but one soul in two bodies."[38]

Whatever disturbed Mario affected Stan. Yet, he felt he had to control himself in order to comfort Mario as he went through one thing after another. Stan spoke of one time when Mario, a Hispanic of Roman Catholic background, wondered out loud what would happen to him after he died: "Then there came a time when he said he didn't like what was happening to him. He knew he was going to die, and he wasn't sure where he was going to go. I said, 'You've never been bad.... You're such a beautiful pure spirit that nothing bad could happen to you.' After that he was very calm. He spent a couple of nights not sleeping at all. We were lying in each other's arms the whole night crying. I guess saying goodbye to each other." Stan's words spoke of what he saw in Mario and enabled his sick partner to feel God's deep love for him through his lover.

As the disease progressed it meant that Stan had to provide more physical caregiving as well. When Mario had trouble breathing, Stan would stack pillows behind him to ease the discomfort. During the last three months of Mario's life, Stan slept in a bed near him so that he could hear him and be right there whenever he called. Very often he would wake and hear Mario's labored breathing. Fearing he would not be able to breathe at all, Stan would get up and pound on Mario's back to loosen the phlegm and clear the passageways. Hardly a night would go by without Stan getting up to help Mario. Deep sleep and a restful night became things of the past.

Throughout, Stan's focus was on Mario's welfare: physical, spiritual, and psychological. Here is the self-transcendence spoken of as an essential part of spirituality. In relationship, partners move out of self to the other and for the other. Not centering on self and isolating themselves within their individual world of pleasures, partners find their wholeness in the other.[39] There is a fulfillment partners discover in being for the one they love. It is such a liberation that they find what they consider to be the real meaning of life: being for the other, an other-centeredness which does not mean that they lose concern for their own future.

HIV/AIDS and Separation

Lou and others saw death entering their lives and breaking what had been so precious to them — relationship. In reflecting on how he felt, Lou said, "In my daily life I began to think, 'I'm going to be alone

one of these days because I'm negative.' There was also a denial process. It's just that all of a sudden death was a reality. The things we
had planned for the future we still talked about, but I think we both
knew they wouldn't happen." The need to maintain hope provided
the means for both to continue and to face what was happening to
them as best they could.

In the relationships we are considering, HIV/AIDS exerted a constant presence. Chris spoke of this as a daily difficulty. One had "to
deal with that presence or knowledge every day, trying to maintain
a comfortable level of denial." Claude and Shaun were both seropositive. Claude said, "It's always — yes, always, always, always
there. I dream about it. Most of my dreams are about HIV, and that
I find very annoying. I wish I could change that part, but. . . . " You
find that you cannot escape the presence of HIV or AIDS; at the
same time, you cannot allow it to usurp every moment of each day.
Each person finds ways of living with it, even when outsiders might
consider this denial.

Rick noted the constant presence of HIV too and how it affected
both him and his partner, Phil: "It's always in the back of your mind,
the feeling that you're living with HIV. The most difficult thing is the
tension that arises between Phil and me. A lot of it comes from the
reaction of people to HIV and AIDS. We both get angry at that. I
get angry in general with the injustice and discrimination of people
shooting their mouths off when they're uninformed or emotional."
Rick and Phil found that the anger and frustration could be present
even within their own relationship. This is not unusual, although
partners do not always express it verbally. Some like Rick do, however: "Phil will say, 'You have no idea what it's like living with
HIV.' And I'll get angry and say, 'You miserable little fart. Maybe
I don't, but you have no idea what it's like to live with it the way
I have to live with it. You're my partner and you have it. Maybe
you live with it your way, but I live with it every day as well. It's
a different way than you do, but it's just as real.' " HIV/AIDS affects both in the relationship, and in a relationship where one is
positive and the other negative, each one feels different effects. Rick
verbalizes an important element present in couples affected by HIV/
AIDS. Both partners experience great psychological and emotional
pain, but certainly from different perspectives. The seronegative person deals with the possible loss of someone he loves deeply and with
thoughts of a future which seems bleak and unimaginable without
the one he loves.

Greg describes the feelings of the seronegative partner well: "It was a real trauma for me — call it survivor's guilt. It was really very hard to be HIV negative. The most difficult thing was dealing with the kind of isolation that Al was feeling — a kind of stigma that he was feeling. There were times when he would say, 'You just don't know what it is to be HIV positive until you walk in my shoes.' To me that was the hardest thing. I had to listen very deeply to that and try to process that. I had always seen us as a couple and had tried to process feelings together. I didn't really understand what he was going through. I tried my best and wanted to be very supportive." Not only did Greg have to deal with his own feelings of inadequacy; he also had to face the fact that Al made the separation more difficult by telling him that he did not really know what he was going through because Greg was not seropositive. All this deeply challenged him as lover and caregiver. His choice to continue loving became the place where his spirituality took on flesh.

Sexuality

Whether one or both are seropositive, diagnosis of HIV/AIDS affects the sexual expression of love. For Tom this was a major difficulty in his relationship with Tim. "I'm a very sensual person. When we first got together we had a lot of sex. As years went by I almost refused to accept that he was too tired. It's been a really religious experience for me. I have actually cried during, if not immediately after, because I just felt this great person was there. It seems the culmination of the two bodies is overwhelming. Afterward I have all this energy and drive to do things." To relate sexually less often was difficult. However, Tom handled this by accepting "things as they are and hoping that tomorrow he will feel better. I get very sexually frustrated, and that's when I tend to get angry and say things I might regret." Despite this suffering, their relationship continued to deepen.[40] Letting go of the sexual dimension at times becomes one of the more difficult aspects of a relationship in which HIV/AIDS has appeared. It is something which the partners must deal with consciously as they live their lives of love in a new context.

Sloan and Keith were both seropositive. They noted a change in their sex lives. The drive or even physical ability to do some things they had done "wasn't there anymore. Also, the AZT just seems to target that place in the brain that changes your sexual drive. So our sexual action changed to much more of a 'vanilla' kind of thing. The couple's books say that happens anyway."

Sexuality is an important element in any gay couple's relationship. Indeed, it forms an essential element in their spirituality as well. For spirituality is a lifestyle that includes who we are — body-spirit persons. The sexual language expresses things which cannot be expressed in any other way.[41] We are sexual beings at all times, and to speak our loving intimacy in sexual relating is not only important but essential in a relationship of love. The sexual acts which incarnate love may vary at different times and stages of the relationship. But the love that partners have for each other dies if it is not expressed in some sexual way. The sacredness of sexuality finds its depth in the love two people have for each other.

When HIV/AIDS enters the relationship, that dimension is bound to change. The changes involve adaptations to the situation of medical and psychological differences which have entered the relationship. Gay men in love have found that sexual expression has a myriad of ways to speak love. It may be as simple as a kiss or a hug. Whatever way it is expressed, it comes to be the couple's way of saying in a concrete physical way, "I love you as you are and I am yours." Partners facing HIV/AIDS can call on many ways to keep their sexual love alive.

Partner's Care for Self

Trying to maintain one's own health while caring for the partner who is ill can be a challenge. The toll of caregiving is such that without attention it can render one unable to continue. In providing care for Randy, Frank began noticing that he had less and less energy. As a result, "I began rethinking my eating patterns, and by doing that I've lost about eighteen pounds. I don't think of it as a diet. I think of it as being healthy and being vigilant about nervous eating. I'm seeing a little more of an equilibrium in my energy level because of it. I'm not doing it only to feel good today. I know I'm going to be called to do a lot more to take care of Randy and this way I'll be able to do it." Frank came to see how important it was to remain healthy. This concern for his own health became part of his pursuit of spirituality, for it was essential to the value of the loving relationship he had chosen as central to his whole life.

Ken too "struggled between wanting to care for Lewis and needing to care for myself. I began to recognize that my ability to care for him was being compromised by my depletion of energy. I needed to get renewed and take care of myself and balance myself and balance all of that." Sometimes people can lose sight of what is important and thus destroy the very process they are trying to preserve. Many partners discover in their caregiving that if they are to be the lover they want to be, they have to take special care of themselves. It is that "balance" of which Ken spoke. The balance is difficult to attain because we always fear that maybe we are just not doing enough for our lover. In it all, however, what stands out is the sacredness of the relationship. It is that recognition that carries the caregiving partner along. His love keeps opening him to the other.

Dennis had to consider all this with added problems. Hal had developed AIDS at a time when AIDS services were practically nonexistent. True, they were able to obtain the services of a home-maker, but while the homemaker was there, it was the rule that Dennis had to be out. He couldn't stay at home during those times and take much-needed rest. Everything fell upon Dennis all the more, since he and Hal had kept the diagnosis secret.[42] Dennis notes, "The majority of the time I was catering to his needs. As his condition deteriorated he needed more and more help. He didn't want to go into the hospital.... So, it was just Hal and I together. I was trying to take care of him and the house and deal with my own emotional instability. He got progressively worse.... In the end he was incontinent, and mobility was a real problem for him. Our townhouse was a split-level and the stairs were a real hurdle for him...the bathroom was upstairs. It took him easily twenty-five minutes to get up the stairs. I had to deal with all of that myself." Despite the fact that he wanted to care for Hal at home, Dennis simply could not go on. "Finally, I had to put Hal in the hospital. If I didn't I was going to kill myself."

The struggle to admit one's limitations emerges in such situations. Caregivers often want to do everything themselves. Eventually the realization grows that something has to change. This realization is part of coming to know who one is — a self with all one's limitations as well as potential. Understanding this means that we are entering a deeper phase of spirituality which recognizes our bodily limitations in certain contexts. To live a spirituality means to live the reality which is our particular situation at any given time. Caring for someone we love who is living with AIDS can be the occasion for such spirituality.

All of this means that partners and lovers come to discover the essential element of community in their lives as human beings. The community they discover is not only a support. Rather they discover or simply reaffirm that life is not lived alone or even as a couple.

Moving out to another in love moves us into a community of people who form part of that other's life. Also, we bring to our relationship the whole community which we have engaged in our own lifetime. Our stories are never individual stories but stories of communities meeting, sharing, and contributing to the developing humanity that we all are. Spirituality always accents this communitarian dimension; we are not alone in our becoming and integrating our ultimate values. To find spirituality moves us out of our egotistical self and into a self constructed positively in relationship to others, that is, into community.

Physical Changes

To watch the one you love succumbing to AIDS can be extremely difficult, especially as you realize that there is nothing you can do about it. Over the weeks and months, subtle changes become more pronounced, and you are forced to see what is happening, even if previously you were in denial to avoid the failing process occurring in the body of your lover.[43] Harry notes his difficulties saying, "Personally, the most difficult thing was to watch him age. He was one of the prettiest men — he was only thirty-three when he died. To watch him in a period of about fifteen months and especially in the last four months, to see him turn into a man who had the face of a thirty-three-year-old man and the body of a seventy-year-old — this was extraordinarily difficult. The wasting syndrome was the hardest part."[44] The only thing Harry could do for Bobby was to cook, but soon Bobby developed diarrhea and would immediately lose whatever he consumed. With that Harry's own appetite disappeared, "Then I couldn't eat. I became almost anorexic. It made me sick to look at food." A friend would force him to go out with her to eat. To deal with it all Harry "stayed sober, which was surprising, but that's because I knew that I had to be. I kept a lot of my feelings inside. I tried to create a kind of normalcy as far as possible. It wasn't always interesting. Sometimes all Bobby wanted was to have someone sit with him and watch TV, which isn't always my kind of thing to do. We might not say a word."

In Harry's story and in the stories of all these men who loved, we discover what asceticism is really about. Asceticism is not some perverse way of dealing with the body through fasting or living on a mountaintop. As an integral part of a spirituality of wholeness, it is a letting go for the sake of another, of the community, and of humanity. Each man in this book gave up time, things he liked to do, freedom, and a thousand and one other things so that his lover could have just a bit more ease, peace, and comfort. This is the spiritual discipline needed to continue the journey toward full integration of love in one's life.

For Rico, the changes brought about by the deterioration of Jon's condition meant establishing a new routine of care at each stage. "Everything came in steps: bringing him to the hospital for the first time; putting a diaper on him for the first time; having a wheelchair come into the house; having seats for the tub and seats for the toilet bowl; handlebars and the hospital bed...step, step, step....I knew what I had to do each day. The minute I woke up I would go into his room and change whatever needed to be changed and make him comfortable. Then get the laundry going. There was always laundry. There was always something to do. Try and stimulate him enough so that he could wake up. Feed him and on and on. Every day it was the same: change his position on the sofa, change him. Then at dinner time, it became a real routine. Every day was the same. Then around 7:30 or 8:00 o'clock I just decided I couldn't go on anymore. He had his TV and everything." The routine was boring, but necessary. Fatigue filled Rico. Yet, he went on because he loved Jon. Rico discovered himself, his limits and abilities, in caring for Jon.

Demands of the Lover

During the progression of the disease, the lover sometimes makes demands which create difficulties for the partner who is caring for him. Such demands can even be a way of keeping control when everything else seems so beyond one's power. When Jason and Karl moved west, Karl's illness accelerated. They had just moved into their apartment and had not even unpacked everything. Jason did not want to unpack. He thought Karl would die at any moment. Then Karl said, "We need to have our home. We need to have a home. How can I feel comfortable if you can't?" Jason said in reflecting on this, "I had to learn to trust. I had to learn to let go." Later Karl told Jason that he would die soon. This made Jason upset; he didn't know what to do. Finally, Karl told Jason to quit his job and take care of him. Jason felt this was not reasonable, but Karl simply said, "Sometimes you just have to have faith and trust. Just trust." Jason did quit his job, and he gradually let go of worries about where the food and money would come from. "I learned to appreciate the moment and how important a choice was," Jason said, "that if you didn't make a choice the choice would be made for you." The whole experience enabled Jason to relax and to express what was happening to him: "I became more comfortable in my life as a gay person. I was never comfortable with showing my sexuality in public. I just learned to be more comfortable."

Jean found that Alf, though very ill, tried to take on big projects despite his illness. He insisted on buying and renovating a house. "What it did to me — it just increased my workload; increased my worries, even took away some of the precious time we could have had relaxing instead of working." And yet, Alf depended upon Jean "for almost everything... but in the end it became very heavy, very heavy because how do you work full-time and take care of someone full-time and worry all the time." What pulled Jean through was love. "I had never loved somebody like I loved him, and I had never been loved like that in my own life."

Paul found that as Grant became bedridden and developed dementia, he "was very demanding. There was always only one way in which anything should be done, and it was his way. It wasn't always the same way to do the same thing each time." Yet, despite the frustration it caused Paul, he tried to do the best he could. He survived by getting away to have his space and getting support from Grant's associates at work and some priest friends.

For Duncan, "The one most difficult thing was Cliff's not wanting me to be outside the household — other than my work. And he resented that too. He resented the church [Duncan's employer]." To be limited to the house when it was not necessary became a serious problem for Duncan, yet through therapy "and by screaming sometimes when it got too much," he was able to handle it.

Others' Reactions

It was the reactions of other people, including family members, that caused Duane the most difficulty. "I have a sister who won't let us come to her house because she's afraid for her family. That hurt me tremendously."[45] There were the friends who had said they would help but who because of fear "turned their backs." Ignorance and fear create problems for those most intimately involved with HIV/AIDS. These problems become challenges for the partners to dare to live authentically no matter what others think. Painful as such experiences can be, they can be opportunities for gay lovers to authenticate their lives and their loves.

Loss and Religion

Jess, a man of Asian background raised within the Roman Catholic tradition, became terribly stressed by two great fears. First, the thought of losing his partner, Max, pained him tremendously. "I felt frightened. I felt afraid that he would die and that I would lose him, that the relationship would end, that I would be alone in this world." The fact that both were closeted and not really part of the gay community in their city deepened that fear. The isolation Jess felt overwhelmed him. Second, during the time of the relationship as well as during Max's illness, Jess lived a traditional, if not conservative, religious life. Max's atheism created a fear in Jess that if Max died, "he won't be saved." However, Jess gradually changed his way of thinking; he described his attitude at the time of the interview in the following way: "My notions of death, heaven, hell, spirituality have all completely changed now. But at that stage, that is where I was at."

The religious formation which Jess had received was at the root of both his fears. Homophobia prevented both him and Max from being open about their deep love for each other. Society's deep-rooted fear and even hatred of gay men made Max and Jess remain in hiding. Homophobia made them lead inauthentic lives, which in turn made it impossible for them to develop a deeper spirituality.

Ecclesiastical homophobia was the cause for Jess's other concern about Max's "salvation." Jess understood the teaching of his church to mean that without believing in God one would be condemned to hell, and the homophobic condemnation of gay persons by that same church augmented Jess's fear that Max would be beyond the pale of salvation. The pain these ideas caused Jess can be really understood only by someone who has experienced the oppression created by homophobia in both society and church. It was only after Max's death that Jess was finally able to come to grips with himself as a gay man and his relationship with Max. A Roman Catholic priest and some friends helped Jess not only to see, but to affirm as good, his sexual orientation. Jess came to see how his relationship with Max had been not only good, but part of God's loving care for both of them. Since that time Jess has developed a deep gay spirituality, the basis for a life he did not think he could ever have as long as he feared his sexuality so much.

Feelings of Powerlessness

Very often AIDS seems to control everything in the life of the people
involved. Ronald noted, "I would call the house from work to see if
he needed something," and he would think twice before taking any
commitments for fear that Kerry, his partner, might get ill.[46] He even
put his professional career on hold: "I was so 100 percent sickness
that I had no time for myself. I had to step back and see where I was,
what I had done, where I was going. It was also the pain. I wanted
him to be freed of that pain. It was the powerlessness, the feeling of
helplessness that I could not help him and do more. But I couldn't."
Feelings of powerlessness may cause the partner to cry out in despair or anger, raging against God or whatever might be controlling
their lives. Such cries can also be a plaintive plea for help. Those
cries, whether verbalized or not, can become the occasion for the
partner to stand back and look at what is happening — both to him
and his lover — not only physically, but psychologically and spiritually. In following through that call, the partner may find a thread of
hope and a way to live out the painful hopelessness which fills such
situations. Following through will also provide new life for the relationship which has endured all this. The spirituality of partners as
individual lovers and particularly as a couple can find a new depth
which provides added strength to live out whatever it is that their
lives together will entail in their journey with HIV/AIDS.

Preoccupations and Worries

As we have seen, to be involved with HIV/AIDS, especially as a
partner whose lover is ill, means to be confronted with all kinds of
concerns. The partner may wonder "How I can take care of him?"
Or "What will happen to us?" There might be worries about finances or one's own health, especially if the caregiving partner is
himself seropositive. Any number of issues may present themselves
throughout the progression of the disease. Each becomes important
to the caregiving partner. What they are and how they are handled
give us some indications of the spirituality which each of the partners
tries to live.

Concern for the Other

One of the most common worries emerging from the stories recounted in this book is the concern for the partner who is infected

or ill with AIDS. Whether the concern is for their lovers' deteriorating health or about dealing with new stages of the illness, partners find themselves daily confronted by this preoccupation. Each day partners awaken with a gnawing feeling in their stomach, wondering what will happen that day. Every change in his lover's ability to do certain things worries the partner. If his lover sleeps later than usual, he wonders if that should signal a more careful observation. If his lover mentions that he feels different, the partner may become afraid. There is no way around it. The only thing he can do is try to encourage his lover and then to live with him their day-to-day lives, hoping that the problem is just ordinary fatigue or flu. But when alone, the partner finds fear coming back to haunt him. The ghost of HIV/AIDS becomes his constant companion. Somehow he has to try to let the worry go and hope.

Rico focused on making "sure that Jon was as comfortable as possible and that he was safe too. My ex-lover was in a hospice. It was a nice place, but I couldn't stand the thought of me being here and Jon in the hospice. He was a special guy for me. The trust he put in me, that he gave me. Even when I think of it, that's what hurt me the most I think.... I always said one thing, 'I've got to try and make the best of it.' And I think I succeeded. I had to — you know on a tough day you had to laugh too. That's the only way to get through it.... Some funny little thing like putting three cigarettes in his mouth. He had a habit every night: when I'd take him to the sofa, I'd bring him out of the room and he'd grab on to everything in his path, the chair, the doorway. He'd have a big smile like a baby — it gave me strength." The joking made it easier, but Rico says that he just had to do "whatever I had to do. I made him as comfortable as possible. I felt abandoned, lonely, frightened — all kinds of things. But I also felt joys too." When Jon was very ill, Rico went to a community center to find help. But he couldn't talk once he got there. "I almost had to prove my sanity to them. I really got scared. I thought they might have the power to take Jon away from me." The fear of being judged incapable of caring for the one he loved forced Rico to take hold of himself and move on — caring, while providing the best image he could so that they could stay together. Rico's spirituality was not ethereal, nonbodily. His worries about Jon made him focus outside himself, feeling all the joys and suffering that their life together involved. His spirituality was living out his life with Jon and all that it contained.

Seeing his lover suffering became a constant preoccupation for
Cyril: "His suffering and pain worried me, that I could not keep
him in comfort, that it would kill me or that I would get sick myself and not be able to take care of him. I didn't sleep much during
those months. From June to August 27 I was sleeping only three or
four hours a day. No sleep, and my nutrition wasn't the greatest."
Cyril has no idea where he got the strength to do all he did. He
says, "I didn't have time to deal with feelings.... I was still drinking
a lot. I would go hide myself in the washroom or in the shower and
get a good cry out for about fifteen or twenty minutes." His lover's
condition created havoc with Cyril's own physical health. Sometimes
only drink seemed to help. The bouts of crying and thus confronting
his anguish were important elements in his coping. They actually
helped Cyril to be there for his lover. As such they formed part of
his spiritual path.

Frank found that he was constantly concerned about Fabian's
pain. In addition there were "the hassles we had with the doctors.
Mind you, one of them was very sensitive to the issues. But prior
to that they didn't seem to believe the pain he was going through.
He finally said, 'All I want is something to control the pain' — and
that was months and months before he passed away. After he said
that, he decided to stop eating. He was quite comfortable, and it
was a natural thing for him to do. No matter what I would do
to get him to eat, it would not happen. He was not hungry. He
would take his pills. All he wanted was the medication to prevent
the pain." Frank cried a lot someplace where Fabian would not hear
him. While he had support at his work, Frank was a person who
preferred to "take care of my own feelings." To handle the situation,
he would go to a large, beautiful park overlooking the city. "There's
a look-out there... you sit on the cement edge and the world seems
pretty far away. I did that twice. It helped." To realize the beauty of
nature and take time to be part of it formed an important part of
Frank's spiritual practice. It was his way not only of regaining balance, but of feeling connected to the world outside bed pans, pain
killers, incessant laundry, and sadness.

Watching the one you love suffer fills the daylight hours and
drains energy from you as caregiver. For Ron, seeing Kerry in such
pain made him feel powerless. "It was the powerlessness that preoccupied me.... It preoccupied me in my work. I didn't do things in
the same way. It was always fast, fast, fast. To spend as much time as
possible with him.... He was first. What did he want? If there was

something he wanted, if there was something I could do for him, I would do it." Yet, Ron also had to deal with his sense of helplessness. The experience of his limitations and the need to let himself rely upon a transcendent power or at least upon others became clear. The whole experience forced Ron to see his own limitations.

Greg put it very succinctly: "If Al was worried about pain, I would worry about his suffering. I was also worried about losing him. I wasn't sure I could live without him. Al once said to me, 'I think it may be time for me to take my life.' His health was diminishing, but I asked him not to do that to me. I was very concerned because I had to go away that weekend. That was one of the hardest things to deal with. I didn't want to see him suffer as much as I had seen others suffer." Though Al did not commit suicide, Greg remained deeply concerned about his suffering and tried to alleviate it. Whatever one partner lives affects the other. The two are inseparable because of their commitment. The spirituality of one partner is in the spirituality of the couple, for they are one. This means that the noninfected partner finds that his spirituality has to encompass the progressive loss of a key element in his life. He must deal with it and allow his lover to go. Pain, loss, and anguish become feelings which create new strengths and new ways of living.

Whatever can help becomes the overriding focus in the battle for a decent life. It becomes the partner's life. His own reality or material concerns are quite secondary. When the partner does something for himself or in his work, he does it to be able to continue to care for his lover. Moreover, such concerns provide a way of dealing with something over which one has no control. Some might call this denial, but in reality it is survival and a search for a worthwhile life for both the caregiver and the lover who is ill. It is in this very predicament that spirituality is found — a way of life centered upon the other who is one's all-encompassing value. Even prayer, when it happens, is centered on the other's well-being and one's own need for strength to comfort and love the other more deeply. Obsessive? Maybe. But also the stuff of deepening life and love.

Keith and Sloan, both seropositive at the time of the interview, were worried about each other, as were Claude and Shaun.[47] Keith said he was concerned about "how Sloan's going to deal with going on drug therapy. I'm not sure mentally how he's going to handle it, nor how his body will handle it. His body metabolizes it really hard. I was on six or seven pills a day. I'm not sure his body is going to handle that." Sloan feared the relationship ending. "I just don't want it to be over with. And I don't want to find myself alone again. . . . I'm more afraid. I don't want him to suffer." He went on to say, "One of the characters we love in *Designing Women* is the one who had been the beauty queen all her life and seemed to be so helpless. At one point she and her sister move in together. Suddenly Suzanne, who was always the Southern flower, is taking charge and is helping out. My hope is that in a crisis I would be like Scarlett O'Hara. But the process is so frightening. . . . I'm afraid for his suffering and for me."

Variety of Worries

Some partners felt failing health occupied them most. For Chris, "the major preoccupations were health concerns. I had Phil exercise. I made breakfast a main meal, not rushed." They both tried to keep abreast of new therapies. Chris found that he became constantly worried about Phil's health. During the last year of his life, there seemed to be a new crisis every week. There was the CMV infection, which caused Phil to lose his eyesight, and an emergency appendectomy. These took their toll on Chris, who couldn't escape his fear of losing Phil. Jack worried about the insurance. "One of the things that preoccupies me is the god-damned insurance prices." They had their medical insurance through the state in which they had maintained their official residence; Jerry could not get insurance in any other place because of his preexisting condition.

Jason worried that "I would die before Karl did because I wasn't sure that I could maintain that pace of life for an indefinite period of time." Sloan feared both Keith's death and his own becoming ill. "I think I get more afraid than he does. I'm afraid of getting sick and I'm afraid he'll die. We had to go through so much to find each other." Steve, who was a Native American, felt the terrible void that Sean's death would leave in his life and feared "that he would die when I was alone with him. I was afraid of that. I don't know why. I felt a part of me would die with him. But the biggest fear was that I would be alone with him when he died."

Harry was worried "that I wouldn't be able to take care of Bobby. He never got to that point. One of the things I did was to insist that he take care of himself insofar as he could. I refused to do things he was capable of doing. One time we had a horrible argument about it. I said, 'Bobby, when you get to the place where you can't do that anymore, I'll do it for you.' One of the most moving things that happened to him was when he was last hospitalized. Supposedly, he was still going to go home. He looked at me and said, 'Harry, I can't do it anymore.' I said, 'I know. We're going to take care of it together.' I'll never forget it."

Duncan worried about "the practical things. You know like changing diapers in the middle of the night. That sort of thing. Getting Cliff to the hospital when he needed to be gotten there even though he wouldn't go. Then he'd get violent or — not exactly violent, well, he was some — but he was basically stubborn.... And my worry was 'How long?' One of the worries I had was how long was this going to go on and how much could I take? Even with my commitments to him." And Darin had similar feelings: "Emile was difficult to live with when he was going through the dementia and wasn't medicated — because he was so different. But I just wanted to do my best and be there for him. That was my biggest fear, that I wouldn't be able to see it through."

All the worries wove the web of these caregivers' lives. They couldn't escape them. These were a daily reality that had become their lives. Whatever their worries, they were all basically concerned for the well-being, the nonsuffering of the other — or at least to help the other get through it the best he could. The love they shared made them live one life together. When one was in pain, so was the other. Love creates such inescapable unity. Their lifestyle was centered upon the wholeness of the other and their relationship, even when disagreements arose. The sum of it all was their spirituality, concrete and enfleshed in their lives.

Experiences of Crises

As AIDS progresses, a toll is taken not only on the lover who is ill, but also on the partner who provides the caregiving. Stan described the horror of the last months of Mario's life: "The last couple of months I couldn't think clearly because I couldn't get enough sleep. I would just get to sleep and he would need me for something. Then it would take me an hour to get to sleep, and he would wake me again. I remember thinking, 'If only I could have a sleep-through, I'd be fine.' After several nights of this I would get desperate. I remember thinking if I prayed hard enough and did things right maybe he wouldn't die, but emotionally I couldn't face it. I didn't even want to let myself think about it. I thought the thought-waves might have power themselves, and I didn't want to let even that much negativity in."

Ricky had had a number of seizures and had lost his speech. Jake noted, "He'd sleep during the day, and at night he would be up and down. All night I couldn't sleep. I was basically home. I couldn't go out because I couldn't leave him alone. I had some friends come over every once in a while so I could get out of the house. Nurses were supposed to come and help wash him. Sometimes they didn't show up and they didn't call. It just drove me crazy." The last two weeks Ricky had seizures and high temperatures day and night. Every little thing began to get to Jake. Having little sleep, he was very irritable: "I was feeling that I wish I could control this, but of course you can't. I had no control. Ricky always had to be doing something. He always had to help. He came in and was putting the coffee pot away. He broke it. I snapped and yelled at him, 'Please don't help.' He wasn't talking at the time and I don't know if he understood the tone." Though it is natural to lose your temper in such circumstances, you do not want to hurt the one you love, especially when he is so ill. This becomes yet another burden for the partner as he comes to see clearly how limited he is. It is in this realization that his spirituality must be worked out.

All of the difficulties can build up to a point of total frustration. Chris spoke about this as he described having to drive Phil to the hospital: "Usually I wouldn't squeeze things in, but I was frantic and I was supposed to drive Phil over there to the hospital. Some guy cut me off and I became obnoxious and then Phil got upset with me.... I lost it! That was the day I cried, and I lost it for a while. Most of the afternoon, I was crying. I was totally devastated and overwhelmed by the constant barrage of things and having to deal with them all. You just live on the edge constantly." Often, even if there are home care and visiting nurses, it is the partner who has to be there, sometimes trying to juggle work with caregiving, seeing to the proper medications, cooking, cleaning, scheduling medical appointments, trying to handle his own fears of what is happening to his lover as well as to their relationship, and, just as importantly, what is happening to himself.

Greg's crisis came when his lover Al was dying in the hospital. Greg's own brother also had AIDS. "The day my brother died from AIDS, I thought I was going to come apart. My doctor wanted to prescribe tranquilizers, but I didn't want them. I felt everything was lost. I felt powerless. It seemed the world was falling apart, but I also felt I needed to be there with Al. My two worlds were coming apart." Torn between wanting to be with his family because of his brother's death and wanting and needing to be with Al meant making a heartrending decision: going to be with his family or staying with Al. He couldn't leave Al alone despite the blood ties.

In the early years of the epidemic, Dennis found that not only Hal's condition but also the health care services created difficulties for him. "Hal was now bedridden on the second floor of the apartment. The meningitis had spread up the spinal column and into the brain. He was not really aware of who I was. That was very hard to deal with. It was driving me crazy." After a lot of searching a palliative care group offered two weeks respite, but Dennis had to sign papers saying he would be back in two weeks to take Hal home. After he came home again, Hal thought he was still in the palliative care home and would yell out, "Nurse, Nurse!" "I would go upstairs, over and over," Dennis said. I was just so exhausted. I was just a mess. My brother and his wife came from the reserve, and they just looked at me and said, 'You can't keep this up anymore. You've got to get him into the hospital.' I explained that nobody would take him. They convinced me to try something. We got him dressed, and my brother carried him downstairs. It was really hard to do. I was feeling very emotional and that I was abandoning him. He was asking me where we were going. I told him we were going for a drive. So I had to be dishonest with him. I got him into the General Hospital. I had to lie to get him admitted. (That's where I learned to lie.) I had to tell them that I just came home from work and that I found him like that and that I didn't know what was wrong with him. I had to deny our relationship once I did get him into the hospital because the doctors were telling me that he was well enough to go home. I knew I couldn't manage anymore with him at the house."[48]

Eventually, Dennis told the doctor they were lovers but that he was not taking him home. "Legally they couldn't do anything to force me because the legal system didn't recognize our relationship. I basically told him to fuck off and leave me alone." This experience was seared in Dennis's mind and he was determined to do something so others would not have to face a similar situation. He decided to establish a center for support as well as to provide a meeting place for persons living with HIV/AIDS and their partners. When Dennis died, the staff, clients, and volunteers as well as his family and other friends filled the chapel for his memorial service.

Cyril's experience was different. Later in the epidemic, attitudes had changed radically for many health care staff. The doctors told Cyril that it would ruin his health to try taking care of Louis at home. But Cyril was determined to try: "When you love someone you can do anything. It gives you so much strength. I think that's what it is — it's love.... Love kept me going. I loved him, and when you love people, there's nothing you wouldn't do for them, even if it means hurting your own self.[49] I even asked Louis if he was afraid of dying, and we talked about a suicide pact so that we would die together so he wouldn't have to die alone. But he was stronger than that."

Rick's partner's count dropped, and his parents were ill. "So a lot of things happened. I think what bothers me is Phil's feeling that says, 'Well, I don't put all of this on you.' Last week he basically said, 'Well, what's the problem? I don't dump all of this stuff on you.' But just because you don't dump it on me doesn't mean it's not there. And really I was at my wits' end...I was feeling helplessness, anger, frustration. I was also feeling, 'Oh, what's the use?' You know the feeling? Also feeling I don't know how much more of this I can take. Although we talk a lot, there's still a gap between him and me. I don't know what he's going through, and he doesn't know what I'm going through. We decided we'll have to talk more about that stuff with each other. But it was a rough month. The HIV has to bother him more than he says it does." Without communication, partners remain islands separate from each other. However, as one expresses his hopes, fears, and pain, he allows the other to understand something of his confusion and turmoil. Sharing becomes a necessary part of the couple's spiritual growth, their life lived in openness to all that is.

It was the last day of Bobby's life, and Harry decided to get Bobby's parents, who lived in another city, to see him. They did not understand how close his death was and how important it was for them to disregard costs and get there. Finally Harry convinced them. "Then," he says, "I realized I couldn't be at the hospital and pick them up at the airport. So I was totally incapacitated.... That really shocked me... but we had said our goodbyes the night before. I realized that Bobby did not need me anymore. What he wanted was his mother to be there." When they arrived, they insisted on going to see Harry and Bobby's house first. Bobby had told them that he wanted that. It was important to him that they see their home. Only later did Harry realize why Bobby wanted them to see it. He had grown up in a tiny house, and he wanted them to see this "splendid three-floor apartment" in a great area where the two of them lived. Then Harry brought them to the hospital. "He died about forty minutes after they arrived. I went out to have a belt of scotch down the street. When I came back he was gone and that was okay. I was absolutely overwhelmed by those last fourteen hours — having to deal with so many things. But you know, I didn't want to sit there for fourteen hours and watch this. I had gone across the Jordan as far as I could go with him."

Crises sometimes precipitate communication, as Jason and Karl discovered. Jason had been running back and forth from the hospital trying to arrange assistance. When he got to Karl's room one day, Karl seemed to be in a coma. He would go in and out of consciousness, sometimes helped by medications. When he was awake he spoke rudely to Jason. Jason had had it. He finally told Karl that he was not acting like the person he knew and loved and that Karl would have to respect him more than that. Karl listened, and they spoke with each other. The discussion brought them much closer together. It opened a strength in Jason to lay things on the table, and it had positive results for their deepening relationship.

For Frank, the last day of Fabian's life was the most difficult. For months Frank had "to carry him up and down the stairs and carry him outside and inside. And near the end he could hardly turn. So whenever I had to clean him, I would turn him. On the last day, and this has been bothering me for a long time, he wasn't sitting up properly in his bed, and I just wanted to lift him up a bit. I went to lift him up, and I just could not lift him up. I had been able to carry him, and at that point I could not lift him up. That really pissed me off, and he noticed it. I said I was mad. I was mad at myself because I couldn't pick him up — not mad at him. When I realized what I did I had to explain to him that I wasn't mad at him, but that I was mad that I just couldn't do it. So I guess I was exhausted and didn't know it. He passed away that night. I couldn't move him that one night, and I got angry." The event became part of Frank's developing spirituality: a sorrow, a letting go, and a remembering.

Past Experience as a Help

All of us draw on what we have lived to face difficulties day by day. This is especially true in times of crisis. We may not realize it at the time, but the past is a source of strength and hope. Life is indeed a school. Every experience, interaction, and relationship leaves an indelible mark on one's spirit. Consciously or unconsciously, we all draw upon those experiences as we face new and sometimes daunting situations in life. Those marks of our past provide us with a way of being in the present which often empowers us with creative means to live out what challenges us. Many of these partners noted this too.

Family Influences

Ken spoke of what might have helped him in dealing with Lewis: "I think of the model of my mother, who trained as a nurse and who set that aside to raise a family. She was always one who cared for people. That image helped as I decided to stay with Lewis full-time." Seeing her concern for others both as nurse and mother influenced Ken, first of all, to enter the ministry and then to be a full-time caregiver for Lewis. The story suggests that it is not in setting out to influence people that we do the most. Rather, it is simply in being who we are that others find in us models for their own lives. People do not always immediately realize how influential others have been in their lives, but upon reflection they sometimes do. What is important is to be as fully oneself as possible, for it is in so being that one constructs not only one's personal life, but the life of the whole community.

Ronald came from a small rural Canadian town. Growing to maturity in such a community taught him things that enabled him to care for Kerry. "The experience from my past life which helped me," Ronald said, "was perhaps my education in the family and also the place I came from. I came from a little town. . . . It's a place where people help each other. My parents were not well off, but with help, we could be fine. On the affective level — on the level of help — that's where I learned above all. My grandparents on my mother's side were persons who gave a lot from their heart, who listened a lot and gave a lot of their time for others. My father is someone who gives a lot of his time for others. . . . The way I was raised, I was ready to care for Kerry." Being raised in an atmosphere of concrete concern for others made Ronald ready to devote himself to Kerry as they journeyed through the stages of his illness. When Ronald moved and settled outside his hometown, he brought the values of his community of origin to his new home and his relationship with Kerry. Ronald's spirituality found its early roots in his family life and his rural community.

Experiences of Death and Faith

Several partners noted that previous experiences of death enabled them to be there for their partners as they became ill and died. Chris spoke of the deaths of his mother, father, and brother, who died after long-term disabling illnesses. He found that this provided him with "a background in the practical medical aspects." Seeing what practical care they required enabled him to know what would happen in very concrete ways as Phil approached death. Moreover, his background in Christian Science gave him the means to develop his own inner reality in the context of love and death while his partner grew more ill.

Stan found that what enabled him to go on caring for Mario was "faith in God....I don't know why this happens....I guess it's the power of love and the power of God speaking to us through incredible things." Love empowered him to be there every step of the way, and faith gave him the conviction that somehow God remained present and part of Stan's and Mario's pain — not as an unaffected bystander, but feeling it with them. For Stan, his love and his God could not be separated; both had been a part of his life even before meeting Mario. And both remained with him through the ordeal of Mario's illness and death — not removing the pain, but enabling Stan to live it.

Lou found similar strength in his faith: "I was a Salvation Army officer before. I have faith and although it has changed and altered and grown, without it I wouldn't have been strong. It was something I drew upon." His earlier religious formation became a source of empowerment. Yet, faith's dynamism reveals its authenticity only when it develops as the human person grows in community. To believe, in a religious context, is not simply to accept dogmas and authoritarian commands. Rather it is a process of living in commitment with a loving God through all the vicissitudes of life. As one comes to trust this God who is involved in one's day-to-day experiences, one's life changes. When life experiences meet faith, neither is denied. The believer may wonder if a compassionate God really exists when he confronts the suffering and death of his lover. His lover's death may crush him.

The believer sees and experiences all this. Faith does not remove those experiences nor does it cover them up. Rather, faith provides the possibility of finding something in the doubts, the fears, the loss — in short, everything that life contains. It may take days of cursing God and being terribly depressed. The process of faith-meeting-life does not find its core element in denying the mystery of doubt, but rather in living it out. The faith of believers enables them, over time, to dare to change and to continue to adhere to the loving God they have come to know in a variety of ways. In such experiences, the spirituality of the child makes way for that of the adult.

When asked about past experiences which had helped him, Greg stated, "Two things: one is the Spiritual Exercises of Ignatius. There's a great deal of freedom there. The other was my experience of mortality which I came to know in 1972 when I spent five months in India. Part of it was working at a mission station of my religious community and the other was in the House of the Dying and Destitute of Mother Teresa. That was my first experience of someone dying." Personally, he had a close call with death on a motorcycle in India. His experiences there with death, poverty, and disease made him want to look at these more closely. Upon his return to North America he "got involved in the death and dying program as part of the pastoral program at divinity school...and with all the death and dying issues in myself. I also got into therapy and death with those issues of anger that I had as a kid. Both of these became good resources for understanding my own feelings and processes." Everything in our lives — the events, the people, the communities, the choices — is connected to faith for those who believe. Faith is not something separate from life as it drops down from heaven. Rather, we find its gift in the concrete elements which make *our* lives. Events, relationships, people, and choices, which intimately form who we are, deepen our faith as they deepen our growth as believing human beings. The interaction of life and faith is such that ultimately they become one reality, one source, one life.

Greg notes this: "I can't overestimate the importance of faith there — of Jesus' companionship in my life. That companionship matured into a real love relationship with Jesus. I've always had a very strong sense of his presence, and that has been nurturing and strengthening. It's been very important." Again we see a development caused by the experiences in one's life. To separate life and spirituality is to deny the very heart of both.

But life and spirituality also need to interact in communication. No one lives alone. We share everything we are and have with others — with the community. In sharing we awaken to new dimensions and thus move into new growth as human beings. To live together is a dialogue, a dialogue of life. Greg found that both he and Al had developed good communication skills, which helped him to cope during Al's illness. Experiences of death, reflection, faith, and communication provided the tools of living in the context of a partner's illness and death due to AIDS.

Knowing death as part of one's life experience plays an important role in being able to live through yet another death — particularly that of one's lover. Jack said, "My brothers and I were orphaned when we were very young. My parents didn't die together; they died about a year apart. My mother died of heart failure. She had always been sick and had had open heart surgery. I think the experience of seeing her go through that kind of illness made me see that people can get through things. The result might not always be what you want it to be, but people get through things and life goes on. Being young and having a mom who was sick and who eventually died taught me that life is what it is and you've got to really go for what you want. I always had that feeling; . . . now it's been reinforced. Life is short. You don't have to be frivolous, but you certainly should take advantage of opportunities because you might not have them again. Go for it."

Rick found that the experience of his mother's death from cancer helped him cope when Phil became ill. "But I don't think there's anything that can really prepare you for this. The feeling is still very much that HIV and AIDS are a death sentence." He felt that the hope which often is there for persons with cancer is not present for persons living with AIDS. For him, the experience of Phil's illness was different and frightening.

Caring for Others

Some had previous experiences of caring for others that enabled them to do the same for their lovers. Frank said, "I've always cared about people. So I've always taken care of people, especially my children when my wife left with this other guy and left the children. For quite a few years I was on my own as a young father. It was quite difficult. I learned a lot of things, and one of the biggest was the dependence that some individuals have on me as a human being. . . . I realized that every individual needs some kind of support, that no one can go it alone no matter how much they think they can. There is always something that they will need, and I decided to be there for that special thing."

Other Life Experiences

Dennis also found that life experiences gave him strength. "The strength that I had from being who I am and the experiences I've had throughout life helped me. There were situations I look back on now where I had to be strong and self-reliant. That's what helped make me who I am and that's what I used to get me through." It is interesting that both Dennis and another partner who said similar things about being self-reliant were Native Americans. His independence made it possible for him to deal with all that entered his and Hal's life as Hal became progressively ill.

Duncan found that his father's inability to confront his mother's illness created a difficult period of time in his relationship with his father. "So Cliff's diagnosis and his unwillingness to confront it were like the same sort of thing." Duncan had seen denial before. Now he could recognize it and deal with it.

Sloan had studied process theology in college. He was interested in the problem of suffering. "When AIDS started to hit in our region in 1984–85, I had to make sense of it." He wrote some articles for a pastoral care journal. He was very close to his grandmother, and her illness kept him "face-to-face intellectually and maybe emotionally too with the whole question of life and what we do to keep going."

Perhaps we can sum up this section on what was helpful to partners from their past life experience with Jason's comments: "I finally understood that everything I had been through prepared me for this. Even if I said I was sick of my life, it was being sick of the life that prompted me to choose, to choose where I was. . . . Life was so full, and I was so aware of everything." Life itself is the school where we learn how to live as human beings, fully alive even in the face of tragedy and death.

HIV/AIDS is indeed a journey into a dark night which comes on those who enter it with a vengeance. It brings with it fear, doubt, and a bewildering array of other feelings which conspire to tear apart everyone in its path. Perhaps this is why some people refuse to be tested for HIV. When one is positive, nothing can ever be the same again.

This dark night becomes the initiation of the whole gay community into a spiritual journey — a journey of searching and incarnating what is best in us. Here is its paradox: while it crushes and defeats, it contains the hope of a new life which does not eliminate the past, but incorporates it into the present moment. Depending on how we live out this terrible reality, it can open onto new insights which give life deeper meaning.

This does not remove or lessen the suffering. The anguish of seeing one's lover in pain or his being so different because of the illness may actually increase, as it becomes one's own suffering as well. The partner bears this in his own body, as it sears its reality into his spirit. All the stories we have heard bear testimony to this.

If not during the actual experience, at least on later reflection, we see that the disease can be conquered in many ways. While there may not yet be a cure, there still can be a healing. Healing may take place as the partners live out the horror together. Or it may come for the person living with AIDS only as he approaches imminent death — expressed in his calm, his acceptance and willingness to continue the journey of discovery beyond what the rest of us see as the end of all possibility. It may come for the surviving partner as he mourns not only his partner's death, but the death of some part of himself as well.

To find meaning in lives cut through by the tragic entry of AIDS remains an individual process in the social context of human existence. Beyond and yet within this experience lies the key to spirituality, both for a partner and his lover. It is their love that provides the meaning from which other meanings flow. When some caregivers speak of shallow or failed relationships in their previous lives, they note that they have come to see that the love they now receive and give in relationship with their lover is life for them. Perhaps shallow or failed relationships were such precisely because people simply go through life, rather than experience it, rather than live it. It is love which now grounds them in the present — a present to be lived ever more fully. The partners we have seen dared to allow themselves to be fully present to the whole reality of life as they were given it.

Chapter 4

Values and Development

For all of us, wholeness is found by following our chosen path to its very end. While we may hope that the final result will be positive and will conform to what we've imagined, there are no guarantees about our life. The best answer to the question "What path shall I take?" is "The path which your heart shows you." The only way to know is to choose and to act upon that choice. Every human being discovers the unfolding of the self in the very living out of that self in authenticity. That self is the heart of the person, pointing the way one must follow to become truly and fully the human being one is meant to become.

For gay men the life path can be no other than following who we are and risking all that we are for the sake of the other. In doing so, we embrace the exile.[50] Through fidelity to the unique story that we are and have been given in the face of mystery, we find what makes us whole. Knowing that our humanity is essentially tied to our sexual identity, we discover that our acceptance of who we are as gay men goes beyond mere acceptance. We affirm and celebrate the gift of the totality of our being, which includes our sexuality, our attraction to other men, and more.

I discover such gifts in my interaction in life — with people, with the earth, and with the mystery: all inseparably intertwined. While the sum total of myself is more than just my gayness, being gay colors all that I am. I am on the path that will bring fulfillment the moment I affirm this "I" that I am and am becoming. This "living out who I am for myself and an other" becomes the place of coming to know the self I am. It is only in interrelationship with an other that I find the mirror which gives me the possibility of seeing the one I am becoming as a person who belongs to a community.

As I honestly look at the one my story shows me, I see that I am going where I am sent. Certainly, it is my choice to move in this or that direction. Yet, I also realize that something (or someone?) else is intimately involved in this whole process in which I am engaged: something/someone that I name mystery in life. Claiming the process with all its relationships — both its good components and those less than good — I gradually find my core self, the heart hidden within the shadows of inauthenticity. These shadows develop when I refuse to be who I am and claim my wholeness.[51] Yet, our shadows are not simply to be rejected. They are signposts pointing to the pursuit of something worthwhile, something that provides meaning not only for me, but for creation itself. If I look carefully into my shadows, I see the deepest desire of my heart. This includes but goes beyond all the elements which have made up my life, my being until now. In my core self I find desire and passion for life, and more. I find awe at the magnificence of creation, and still more. It is that more which provides the catalyst for the generativity of life which I as a gay man am capable, as I engage in the creation of self, of others, and the world. In pursuing my "more," I create the world with and in mystery.

Each of us verbalizes our "more" in different ways, ways born of the concrete circumstances of our lives. Within my own life I find the "more" which keeps nagging at me as I pursue it (or try to avoid it). Regardless of whether my pursuit is conscious or enjoys absolute clarity, ultimately I find that this is really the way for me. Paradoxically, following the path with its unclarity remains the only way to clarity. As I walk even in shadows, I integrate and make my own my all-encompassing value. This moves me to the other and simultaneously to the becoming of my authentic self. There is no end to this becoming. In this dynamic of journey there is only the continuing wonder of discovery as I *live* at each instant all that is my life here and now.

Gay partners of persons living with HIV/AIDS express this value of pursuing oneself in relation to the other in a variety of ways. Seeing this value as truly central, some strive to make it the directive focus of their day-to-day lives. For some, this might result in the attempt to listen more carefully to a person whom they find irritating. This might also include the attempt to discover what it is in oneself that creates such irritation. Or our listening might sensitize us to our own way of interrelating that is sometimes abrasive. Other gay partner-caregivers seek to extend compassion to all beings by developing daily routines that allow them to be aware of the suffering of those with whom they come into daily contact. Often for these gay partners, HIV/AIDS becomes the context of the discovery intensification of a more conscious life centered on these ultimate values, a discovery that occurs within the suffering of AIDS.

Values That Caregivers Bring to Partners

Family

For Duncan, who had been a United Church minister and had also spent time with a Roman Catholic religious order, "the church has always been ultimately important." As a minister, Duncan did not hide his gayness. He notes that eventually "I was told by the United Church that I had to go back in the closet in order to work. I refused to do that." So he moved to a larger city and "looked for work, mostly in social service type things. Typical things that clergy would do." Finding nothing, he ended up working ten years in an office furnishing design firm. Yet the desire for ministerial work would not leave him. Haunted by this desire, he joined the Episcopal Church and was ordained. Previously, Duncan had been married and had a family. As he observes, "kids, family, justice" were concerns which stood at the heart of his life. Through all the shifts in his life, he maintained contact with the family he loved. As he spoke of his family in the interview, the sparkle in his eyes revealed their importance for him. For Duncan, being an intimate part of the development of both his biological and his chosen family was a primary value. Furthermore, wherever he saw people suffering injustice, his heart went out to them and he tried to do what he could to create justice for them. Each of Duncan's core values reveals the importance of relationship for him. These values remained constant throughout his life.[52]

For Frank, "The most important thing in my life was how to have a family with children, which I had for eleven years. I guess beyond that it would be to have someone I could love and who could love me as I am, not 'I will love you if....'" Frank had been married before meeting Fabian, and he had children. Providing for his children's development took center stage for him. He also desired to love and be loved as a gay man — which his relationship with Fabian provided. This did not mean that he valued his family any less. On the contrary, family and his love as a gay man remained his values.

Tom had always seen family as important — not in the sense of marriage and children, but in its core sense, a place of acceptance, security, and love. In coming to be committed to his partner, Tim, he found what had always been important to him: "Family, acceptance of family. I was searching for it for years and never had it. As we've become closer I've received that." The family he found and valued with Tim was not his biological family, but the family which he and Tim established in their life together.

Things and Relationships

While Duncan and Frank had been married and had families, Darin had remained single until he met Emile. "So being single and having a profession, you're into material things." He directed his energies into acquiring what seemed important, but meeting Emile would bring a whole new dimension to his life, as we shall see later.

Stan and Mario "had this plan. I owned a house with another friend. We were going to sell our interest in that property and go to a gay resort area or somewhere else and buy a group of cabins and rent them. We were going to become two groovy old men in the country — have a garden, putter around, and rent these cabins. That was what was going to happen." For Stan and Mario having things was a way to have a life together. It was a way of enjoying the love they had found. At the same time, their friends were important: "We loved our friends. Mario and I used to love to visit friends at their homes in the summer." Things and people, sharing and loving, formed key values in their lives.

What is important may change for some partners after diagnosis, but for Chris and Phil things remained the same. "The most important things remained important after diagnosis: Phil, my relationship with Phil, our home, our life together." Like many others, they saw their relationship as paramount in their lives.

Lou noted that, "most of the things that were important before Kean's diagnosis continued to be important — the friends, the church, our house, the dogs. All these things continued to be important. So nothing really changed dramatically. It just took a different shape." While the diagnosis brought a new perspective to their relationship, the important things remained and deepened.

For some, comfort and material security were important elements before their lovers were diagnosed. Steve "just wanted a nice life, an easy life. It was important to be financially secure. Not having enough money really worried me a lot." Cyril spoke of his goals as "just to have a comfortable home, a nice relationship — a loving relationship, and to have a normal and decent life."

Before Phil's diagnosis, Rick spoke of his values in the following way: "I guess money, getting ahead. Those things were important, also traveling and enjoying life. The children — not necessarily in this order."

Dennis found that before Hal's diagnosis, what was important was "probably just work. I had moved to the city in 1981. I came with my clothes and not much materially. So I think my priorities were to get a decent job so that I could have enough income to get a nice apartment and stuff."

For Rico values were not a priority in his life before he met Jon. "It's like I've only just woken up. What was important then? I don't know. I guess having a good time. I guess I was just existing. I didn't have any real expectations. I was in school and though I'd become a designer, I wasn't taking life too seriously. It was important that people be truthful to me, but it didn't matter how truthful I was to other people." Rico's attitudes before meeting Jon were not all that uncommon. Life can be lived on a one-dimensional level. Most human beings have a tendency just to *go through* life rather than consciously *live it out*. However, when love breaks in, it often brings us a new way of looking at everything and a new passion for living.

Before Kerry's diagnosis, Ronald felt that what was important was to find a person with a good education and financial independence. "That was the biggest thing for me. I wanted to be with someone who had a certain education, who was positive as regards future plans and all that." With someone like that, he could have a worthwhile relationship. But like most of the others, he eventually found that something else was more important.

Career

For many people, success in one's profession is absolutely essential for happiness. Sloan said it this way: "My goal was to make my job placement service work and get me a senior track full-time position. I was still trying to get into a full-time position at the time I learned Keith was HIV positive." Whatever the reasons — security, recognition, development of talents — pursuing a career provides the impetus for life for many people.

Jack and Jerry moved west to establish a business. They "dreamed about getting a business up and running and about getting rich and famous. All those things that people dream about, and we still do. I don't know if anything has changed. It's just that we realize now we're not infallible. The road may be a little more difficult, but we're still on the road to a happy destiny and it's been A-OK." Being together not only as a couple but as business partners made sense to them. It was a chance to try out their talents. If successful, the business would provide them the means to live well.

Ken was in a Protestant seminary, and his partner, Lewis was starting part-time studies when they met. For Ken, a variety of interconnected factors were important before Lewis's diagnosis: "Career, developing identity. I was just coming out at that point. Discovery or rediscovery of my spirituality. Wondering about what really I am called to do and where the studies will lead me." As with most of the others interviewed, even when career and the future it promised were important, these were intimately connected to discovering Ken's real self and how his career would express most authentically the self he was discovering.

Spirituality and Religion

Greg, who, as we have seen, had been a priest in a Roman Catholic community, underscored the importance of spirituality: "My spirituality has been very important in my life and continues to be in our household. The community taught me how to love men and to love humanity. . . . I realized from the experience of our lovemaking and recreational sex that they were two different things. This was all before the days when we learned about AIDS." Finding the meaning of life in service to humanity was the core of Greg's spirituality, his key value. His spirituality integrated sex, love, and life, enabling him to see where things came together to enhance his own life and that of his partner, Al. As Greg noted, in their sexual relationship he discovered the important difference between recreational sex and intimate lovemaking as partners. This discovery led to an ever deeper harmonization between his whole being and his sexuality, a process of integration.

For Jess, on the other hand, with his rather traditional Asian Catholic background, relationship brought challenges to tradition. During his relationship with Max, who did not share his religious views, Jess's values were different from what they would be after Max's illness and death. "I guess my approach was traditional," Jess said. "From the time I sensed that there was something wrong with him I started to go to daily Mass. And part of my prayer at Mass was that Max might be okay and would not die. But there was something else added, that if he did die that he would be saved, that he would have faith." Though Jess treasured the relationship, his traditionalist religious beliefs told him it was sinful. The suffering caused by the clash between what he instinctively knew as good and lifegiving and what his religion told him was evil weighed heavily. And it was compounded by the fact that Jess and Max kept their relationship hidden from most people, though not simply because of Jess's beliefs.

Rather than free him, Jess's religion imprisoned him in fear. After discussions with a United Church minister and a Catholic priest, Jess came to accept his gayness and his relationship. And he could say, "God accepted me how I was and that was fine, but still, I'd say at that time I was still traditionally religious. Even if I felt I could be saved even if I am gay, I still needed to believe in God in order to be saved. So the problem with Max was not that he was gay and that we were in a relationship. The problem was that he didn't believe. That was my concern." Jess's deep love for Max and his religious conviction caused him anguish because he wanted Max to be fulfilled and happy. He thought that without faith Max would be neither fulfilled nor accepted by God.

The night before Max died, around two in the morning, he and Jess talked. "At that time he said something to me. I don't recall the exact words, but in effect he was making me aware that he had faith." This certainly relieved Jess, but he adds, "Now I would say that Max would have been saved anyway. He was a good person. Period."

Faith, as he then interpreted it, obsessed Jess and drove him in fear. Fortunately, through friends and clergy, he was able to move to an interpretation which empowered him to see a loving God who was not the creator of that dogmatic box which held Jess tight from his earliest years.

Claude had been raised in the same Catholic religious tradition, but in a different cultural context, that of Quebec. Still the church presented difficulties for Claude too. One day in the sacrament of reconciliation, he spoke of his committed relationship. He did so not because he thought it was evil, but simply to let the priest know his situation more clearly. The priest refused to absolve Claude unless he broke off the relationship. He told him that if he broke the relationship and still had sex with Shaun, he could receive absolution! Seeing this position as nonsensical and unethical, Claude refused to end the relationship. He loved Shaun, and the continuing development of their relationship remained a key value for him, one he would not deny.

Both Claude and Shaun discovered they were seropositive during their relationship. Claude describes his feelings after diagnosis: "I loved him and I still do. I felt suddenly that this was the last part of my life, like the last leg of my trip. Not that I was going to die soon or he was going to die soon, but I had an obligation to stick with him, an obligation — if not a desire — to be faithful. But it was all a mixture of different things that crossed my mind. About caring for him and — I don't know — trying to be more attentive to what he likes." His desire was to be there always with and for Shaun. Who they were as a couple was paramount as they worked through their relationship in the brief time remaining to them. Claude loved people and spoke of his desire to visit elderly people, especially those who had no one left. "I want to do it for the sake of helping someone and because I know if that person would give me love or affection, I would feel good about it." For Claude, Shaun and their relationship were important, as was bringing others a bit more happiness in a lonely life. Love and compassion were key values which Claude attempted to develop.

Prior to their partners' diagnosis and sometimes their own as well, partners held various values as the core of wholeness in their lives. These included a nice house, career advancement, relationship, spirituality and religion. Usually a desire to share their core values with another was present. For some this may not have been conscious at the time. If we look at what the partners say about the changes which occurred in their value system after diagnosis, during the illness of their partner, or after the partner's death, we find some keys to the values which would later come to dominate their lives and provide either new perspectives or intensification of their core values.

Values after the Partner's Diagnosis

Life Itself as a Value

Before meeting and living with Karl, Jason wanted security. He sought both emotional and financial stability, especially the latter. Two things would change that desire: first, Karl's diagnosis and, second, Karl's challenge to let go and trust, which made him rethink his priorities.[53] Jason said that once Karl died, "Everything changed. I learned not to hold on to things. And so whatever is the time that you have, you need to value it and you need to spend your time doing something you find meaningful. For me, for the last three or four years that has been my work. And now that's changing as I'm looking for other things. And time and life. . . . Life has become something very valuable to me." He came to see that each moment has its own story which tells the person who listens what he needs. Within the framework of the life lived, one discovers the path in which he may incarnate what is most meaningful. With this understanding, Jason lives life with dynamism and a hope which extends beyond the present and yet is found fully within it.

When Dennis moved to the city in 1981 he had nothing, "So I think my priorities were to get a decent job so that I could have enough income to get a nice apartment and stuff." Once Hal had been diagnosed, those concerns became less important. His focus was now on people: "I realized how important people are, especially as you are losing someone you care so intensely for. In the end, his body was still with me, but his mind was gone. I actually lost him before he died. So I realized how important people and relationships are." While Hal was ill, Dennis came to a very deep appreciation of life and relationships. After Hal's death Dennis said, "I love the experiences of life. My Indian name is 'the listener.'" Dennis used this listening quality — which was so evidently intrinsic to him — to observe people and life and to affirm those who came to him for help. Face-to-face with illness, suffering, and death, especially when they involve a loved one, people often turn radically around and reevaluate their story.

Intensification or Addition of Values

As we've seen, before Cliff's diagnosis, Duncan valued "kids, family, justice." After the diagnosis of Cliff's illness, these values intensified and were completed by other values. In response to a question about his values after Cliff's diagnosis, Duncan said: "I would say more, adding a new one...I really had to look at Western medicine and Eastern medicine and came down on the side of Eastern medicine...I also got into healing, which I had not been into before — healing ministry, which I do a lot of." Duncan felt that Eastern acupuncture and massage had great potential for healing. Even if they were not total cures, they enhanced people's lives. With these new insights, the ministry of healing became a value for Duncan. During Cliff's illness, he says, "My relationship to him was paramount. Giving him care was the most important thing I could do. It didn't always have to be me giving the care, but I wanted to provide for his care. Second, I wasn't going to allow myself to become so dependent, so co-dependent, so caught up, that I got ill — which I desperately tried not to do." Duncan saw that a value might even be destructive. So, while he intended to see that Cliff received all the care and love he needed, he did not feel he had to do it all by himself. To have carried the burden alone would have been self-destructive. Then the value would have become a nonvalue.

Frank found that after Fabian's diagnosis his core values of family and the need to be loved as he was did not change but deepened: "It intensified. I have never been loved the way I have been loved by him. Even in death...he told me he had written something for me which he didn't let me see. They read it at the church, and I still have it. If I had any doubts of not accomplishing what I had set out to do, that letter took every doubt away from me. It was incredible." Fabian's letter described how much he had loved Frank as he was. This affirmation gave Frank what he needed at that time.

During Fabian's illness, Frank says, "Since he believed in God so much, I would never put him down or stuff like that. I would show interest.... He was the only thing that was important to me." Whatever could affirm Fabian and enable him to live more happily became key in Frank's life. For Frank, as for Duncan and others, his partner's well-being was uppermost on the scale of values.

For all the partners, the death of the one they loved left a void which had to be lived out. Just as with the dying process, they now had to live out the grief in all its complexities. When asked about changes in his values after Fabian's death, Frank said, "I think the only change that has occurred is that I don't care anymore. The most important part of my life has now ended. I don't care as much as I used to care. I know I back off a lot from responsibilities — any kind of responsibility. And I know I back off. I do the best I can just to prevent myself from backing off, but there seems to be a very low level of energy to be able to fight that feeling. But I know it's happening. So I'll get above that at some time. I don't know when, but I will." To recognize and live out the process is crucial. Frank knew that someday it would be different, and this empowered him to live out his hopelessness as he mourned the loss of the one who was so important to him.

Darin found that his interest in acquiring valuable things changed once he entered into a relationship with Emile. "I think the material things we put in our home were just to allow us to enjoy the times we had." Something else occurred when Emile's diagnosis took place. "This click happened where I made this commitment to him, which was basically allowing myself to be loved by him. The diagnosis happened before I think I was 100 percent committed, but I knew I was committed as much as I was capable of committing myself at that point." Darin discovered how important Emile was in his life and now gave himself totally to him, knowing that before he had not fully allowed himself to be loved and to love in return. The "click" opened the door to the real value of his life — Emile and their relationship.

For Darin, there was not so much a change or an intensification. "We just used our situation to enjoy the time we had as well as we could." He and Emile had a bed and breakfast in their fine home, where Emile could entertain friends as he really wanted. After Emile's death, one of his friends told Darin that in their relationship practically all of Emile's dreams came true. This made Darin aware that all they did together contributed to Emile's happiness and fulfillment as well as his own.

Keith felt that his core value remained the same after diagnosis. "The important thing for me is us, and that's not going to change because of an HIV status. I don't think anything changed." After his diagnosis, he found that he valued his time with Sloan more. "I'm finding that's something that's very precious. I never thought I would say that about anybody. The house is not the same when he's not there. So our time together is precious and very valuable to me." In coming to love each other more profoundly, Keith found his personal development centered on his partner.[54]

Sloan, who had a goal of full-time teaching, discovered a change. But was there a change? "Yes and no.... I think I had come to see I was always in this sort of marginalized place. I've also learned to see that being on the margins has freed me up to do the kinds of work — theological work and writing — which the demands of the tenure track would not have allowed. So I've learned that there's a different way." Early in his relationship with Keith he continued to look for a position. Gradually, he saw that what was important to him was putting down roots and establishing relationship as of primary importance.

Sloan's experience of relationship with Keith enabled him to see how important such commitments are. His focus now is not so much on finding a teaching position as "to value gay and lesbian couples and the commitments gay men and lesbians make to one another as couples in spite of pressure — from outside and within." Although some within the gay community feel that such commitments are unfortunate imitations of heterosexual unions, Keith sees it differently: "The commitment should be to be gay and coupled, to be able to have homes, raise a garden, take care of animals, take care of friends.

And to insist in a very strong way that making those commitments is not imitating heterosexuals. I choose to make a commitment to Sloan because I believe in the relationship.... That's a very strong value."

Something that has become important to Keith and Sloan is a concern for life and the earth. Their commitment and their reflection on it have created a value "that has become stronger for both of us put together as a couple,...a commitment to the value of all life: human and nonhuman, biosphere, geosphere,...a really strong commitment to the environment. Ecological values, commitments to other life forms, and discerning what are healthy commitments." Their life together in the context of HIV has opened them to see the interconnectedness of life and to create possibilities for that interconnection to be enhanced.

What Rick held as important no longer had the same importance after Phil's diagnosis: "I think I'm more interested in my relationship with Phil and friends. And I'm more interested in my relationship with people.... My faith is important — a lot of things that my parents taught me, in terms of how you treat other people, respect for others as human beings.... I think I try to be very conscious of how I treat others: 'Treat others how you would like to be treated.' What I see in people with HIV and AIDS is social ostracism and contempt, whether they be gays or ten-year-old children.... I think, 'Is that how you would like to be treated?' That's what's important to me." Life is relationship. Nothing is without value. Everyone needs to be affirmed in order to find happiness. Rick recognized all this and saw it growing within him, especially in his relationship with Phil.

Before meeting Lewis, Ken valued his ministerial career, gay identity, and spiritual life. In relationship he found even deeper values, ones he expressed as "truth, fidelity, honesty, and loyalty." The basis of healthy relationships is authenticity. Ken and Lewis had committed themselves to a monogamous relationship, and for that to thrive they realized how important it is to acknowledge who they were (truth and honesty). They also felt deeply that sticking with the other through difficult times was essential (loyalty and fidelity).

Change in Values

When Rico met Jon, he found another who changed his life. "He was the first person who gave me a sense of home or safety. The first person I ever felt that with was Jon." As Jon became ill, Rico experienced home running through his fingers like water. In previous relationships, his partner had either died or they had broken up.

Rico had not known that sense of home with these partners. With Jon, "It was the first time I could really be myself with somebody. We weren't rich, but we built a cozy little place together." But the comfort Rico found was not in the house he shared with Jon. He found comfort because "it was the first time I could really be myself with somebody." Jon had become the focus from which flowed an ease with himself Rico had not known before.

After Jon died, Rico found that he could be himself with others. "I try to be a good listener. I let people reach out to me more. I can accept things more. Sometimes I still have a hard time with that. I try to be as true as I can be. I guess that is the biggest change in values." To be authentic became his core value. Through his relationship with Jon, who empowered him to be himself, Rico could claim himself. It bothered him when people lived only to meet others' norms. His experience of relationship had revealed to him that inauthenticity would undermine the healthy development of the person. Only when human beings live out of their *real* core can true interrelationship take place. Otherwise one enters a relationship wearing a mask while the real person remains hidden. In relationship Rico overcame the fear of being who he truly was and became free to love. Jon's gift to him was freeing self-affirmation which changed his life.

Steve, who had seen financial security as important before Sean's diagnosis, felt that the diagnosis changed things. "It made me grapple with more." It forced him to look at more than the comforts money can buy. During Sean's illness he found that love was a powerful factor in life "and that we have inner strengths that we don't know about but that come out only during some traumatic experience." After Sean's death that belief became even stronger. Steve had moved from a material concern with finances to a concern for love as *the* important factor of human life. When the human person comes to realize that we all desire to love and to be loved, love has the potential to become the overriding factor in life.

Relationship

Once Louis was diagnosed, Cyril found that "it was important to try to live each day to the fullest.... We did a few trips together. We went to Cancun, Florida, and a few other places. That was very important to me: to see a little of the world.... The most important thing was to live and to try to be happy. Just to be happy is a big thing. It's the main thing." The trips became the means of helping them find each other and their world in a deepening way. Their shared experiences intensified relationship and brought love to life.

While Cyril had been attracted initially by Louis's physical appearance, this changed as well. Cyril notes that during Louis's illness, "I never stopped loving him. Even though his body was changing. When I met Louis he was very muscular. He was a Native from the West. I stopped looking at the physical and I started looking inside the person. That was a big thing. If I had met him like that before, there was no way I would have even touched him. But it didn't bother me during his illness to hold him, to kiss him, or to sleep with him." Embracing Louis with his body scarred by AIDS, Cyril embraced the whole person whom he loved even more deeply than when they met. Love allowed him to see his lover more completely, finding the core which held everything together. The whole Louis called Cyril to love and he responded.

After Louis died, Cyril continued to live by the principle of living life fully each day. This didn't mean, however, that everything became easy and fun. "Sometimes I was mad at the whole world, but it didn't last very long. But I had to work through that. I got angry and I got upset. I even gave shit to God by yelling at him, 'Why the fuck did you do this?' Too much 'why' is not good. I'm not afraid anymore about my friend God. I can talk to him. I know he listens. He answers me back, not verbally but it comes from somebody else's mouth." Like all those who experience a heartrending loss, Cyril struggles while finding hope and trying to live each day with whatever it holds. His relationship with God has become more homely. His relationship has enabled Cyril to see who he is and to live out the person he is discovering. As a result he can relate to God more authentically. He can be angry with God. Knowing God as friend, he can be himself with God. Cyril has also found that mystery speaks in interrelationship. For one attentive to life, the dialogue with mystery can take place. Louis's life has empowered Cyril with insights from which he can live more authentically. In short, Cyril and Louis's love empowered both to find and live their spirituality more deeply.

When Mario became ill, Stan, who was also seropositive, found that his value became "life in general." He tried to make life more beautiful for others, and this was expressed in his attentions to Mario. "I tried to do the best I could to make Mario happy. I tried to make every day special. If he was in bed, ill during the day, I would get fresh flowers. In the evening I would put candles around the living room and light a fire in the fireplace and then bring him out. It was like the old days and nothing was wrong. I tried to make the house immaculate. He was an immaculate housekeeper, and I went out of the way to do my best. I would have friends stop by and not stay too long. I tried to make things nice for him; that was my main concern."[55] Stan's love for Mario became the core of his lifestyle. But this was not relationship narrowly conceived. Stan's love for Mario permeated all his interactions with others, which took on the coloring of his sensitivity to and passion for Mario.

During Al's illness, Greg found his value to be "primarily nurturing and being there for him no matter what. I was his priest. I really saw priesthood being meshed into that love. It was being there with someone I loved." The change came after Al's death. "Priesthood has not changed; a sense of mission to the HIV community has been strengthened. After I returned, I worked to transform ACT-UP into a treatment issues group. It's now a first-rate organization educating the HIV community on HIV issues in everyday language. I've been working at that and find myself mentoring, nurturing, and encouraging people to stand on their feet." Greg moved from nurturing Al to a deeper involvement in nurturing others. Who he had been for Al affected Greg's whole life, as he lived out that concern for the other to pursue the enhancement of all people's lives. The concern for everyone had always been there, but Greg's relationship with Al so intensified it that he saw more clearly the universal implications of his life.

Whether both partners are seropositive or not, the entry of HIV/AIDS into a relationship creates a context in which both must look at what is important in their lives. Despite advances in the medical field, AIDS remains a terminal disease. This means that both partners are aware that the relationship in which they have invested so much of themselves is threatened. The pressures which HIV/AIDS brings to bear on the relationship cause disruption to that which they hold as vital.[56] Trying to find one's way through the pitfalls which seem to be at every turn is no easy task, and is even more difficult, perhaps, when both partners are positive. When only one partner is infected, the noninfected partner must deal with the possible loss of his partner and the relationship around which they have built their lives. In either situation, the partner lives in a context where everything seems to be crumbling about him. In such a context, questions as to what is important come to the fore.

In such a context, HIV/AIDS forces one to examine the driving force in one's life. The gay men who have spoken here about what they saw as their goals or values sometimes found that diagnosis brought radical changes in their view of things, while others discovered that their core values were still intact, but required further integration.

The experience of letting go of what — in the face of suffering and loss — was unimportant is common to all the stories. Essentially, the partners come to value what contributes most directly to the enhancement of their relationship and the life with each other in the present moment. Everything becomes not simply "my" goal, but "our" goal or value. Material things continue to matter as a means to empower each to enjoy what they have as a couple. Careers come to be seen as means to personal and communal wholeness. What distracts from that wholeness needs to be let go of so that the partners can live more wholly within the context of this disease.

This does not mean that everything is easy. It often means stepping into the unknown. The stories we've heard suggest that such a step in trust cannot be taken if the partners do not have each other as their primary concern. The dialogue and openness involved in maintaining relationship through difficult times contain pain at some moments. However, trusting the love of each other even in times of doubt becomes the bedrock of the partners' ability to pursue their life together in such times of struggle.

As the stories indicate, even when the partners are not conscious of an explicit driving force or value, in their relationship, they are aware of the importance each has in the other's life and the desire to hold on to him whatever the cost. Over time this value may become conscious. Crises collapse nonessentials; the inner person takes precedence over the attractive appearance. In crisis we may find that trust becomes more important than security and control. We may choose the mystery of life which empowers us over the collecting of possessions. We may develop a respect for the other as he is over the desire to remake the other into the one *I* want him to be.

All this leads to a greater appreciation of everything which is. The spirituality at work here is not one focused exclusively on the partner with whom I share my life. Rather, it is focused on two people who see that the drama of their lives together is an intimate part of the world surrounding them. Everything around us contains a story which becomes an essential part of our own story as couple. A rock, the trees, flowers, plants, canyons and plains, sky, sun, light and darkness: all these "live" in our relationship and we live in them. To appreciate the moment with all its wonder and grandeur is to appreciate all as part of one whole. Somehow there is the sense that we are all in this together — the earth and ourselves in a dynamic interplay of life and death, shadow and light.

In this sense, the earth supports us, and our role is to support it in a spirituality which sees nothing as without value. I believe that the partners in this book — each in their own way — found that connection. Yet they found it because they found support in other human beings, particularly in their lovers with whom they established a unique cell in that mystery we call life.

Chapter 5

Communities of Support

Whether we are aware of it or not, every part of our being finds its dynamism in, with, and through others. From the day of our birth, our relationships move us through this process we call *living*. Interaction with others forms us into the persons we are each moment of our lives. All that we are and consequently all that we do flows from this formative interaction.

Yet, life is not a one-way street in which we are passively molded by such interaction. For our own being and doing modifies the being and doing of others with whom we come into contact. We are not determined by our circumstances and the people we meet without being able to change what happens. We can choose to enter the process of interaction and thus consciously effect changes. It is *we* who decide the direction of our lives. In pivotal decisions, *we* deliberately attend to our own development as persons.

From the earliest moments of our lives, we engage ourselves in such a developmental process. Sometimes we do so unconscious of the choices we are making. At other times we have clear knowledge of our choices and at least some of their implications. To mature is to become aware of our interactions and to move thereby into some type of developmental change with others like us, in the same humanizing process. Mature human beings know that their lives are inextricably linked to others. The more conscious we become of this, the more consciously we can determine the process of our lives and enhance it in a mature way.

What all this means is that we are never alone in being who we are. Especially with our parents, our biological families become a first line of interaction in which and with which we start to live. Through them we are rooted in a history of people who affected and were affected by their own times and relationships. All these people are not simply ancestors totally separate from us. They form part of who we are. Their blood runs in our veins. In a very real way, they are our roots in life.

Several years ago, I came to know a distant cousin in Canada. One weekend when he invited me to visit his family — and other relatives including cousins and brothers and sisters of my grandfather — I decided to seize this opportunity. I was not very long in Quebec, where most of them lived, before I realized that what I had thought were traits particular to my aunts and uncles in the United States were in fact family traits, part of the one family called Hardys. I had a very similar experience when I visited other parts of Quebec to spend time with the Parents, who made up my mother's side of the family. They might be more "serious" than the fun-loving Hardys, but I could see how I was very much a part of them too and that these two wings of my family came together in myself.

None of us lives, though, only in biological families. Every one of us also comes to create families of choice, people whose intimate connections with us make of us a unit which one can truly call "family." These are families of friends we have met along the way of creating our lives. Consciously or unconsciously, we have dared to open ourselves to them. The intimacy that results and the risk of sharing ourselves bonds us in ties sometimes stronger than those of our biological families. For gay men and lesbians, these families of choice are very often particularly important. Both types of families create us as the persons we are, while we in turn create them as families and as individuals within those families. Our spirituality is affected by our interaction with both kinds of family.

How partners have related to their biological and extended families of choice is an important element in their spirituality. Let us look at how some have seen these relationships and been affected by them as they lived as gay men whose lives were impacted by HIV/AIDS.

Families: Biological and of Choice[57]

In the process by which we find ourselves, our parents initially move us into a certain self-image which we feel is the self we are. But as we mature we become the authors of our own selves, within the context of family influence as well as that of friends and society as a whole. In our interaction with such influences and the struggle this causes, we ultimately find the real person each of us is. At maturity, the masks we have created or which others have created for us fall away. What remains is who we are.

The partners in this book often spoke of that process of coming to know themselves and to be more authentically persons in their own right. That process, for good or bad, involved parents, siblings, children, friends, partners, and acquaintances. As the partners speak of the importance of these in their lives, they are describing their growth process as human beings and as gay men along with the joys and sorrows which that process necessarily involves. Even when it seems that the process they describe is purely an individual experience, we need to remember that the whole community is part of it. Moreover, the process affects the community surrounding the individual whose growth is being achieved in that community.

Consistent Family Support

One summer I attended Shaun's twenty-seventh birthday party in Quebec. His partner, Claude, had done most of the organizing. Along with about fifteen of their friends, Shaun's mother and father were there — seeing for the first time their son's family of choice. They enjoyed all the celebrations, the jokes (on color and off-color), but were especially impressed by Shaun and Claude's friends. Shaun's mother said, "I now see what wonderful friends you have, and I am really comfortable knowing they are with you."

When Claude became very ill and was hospitalized, Shaun's mother and father came to support him and help care for Claude. Shaun's father, who had an intense dislike of hospitals, not only visited Claude, but spent the whole night on a cot next to his bed so that Shaun could go home and get much-needed sleep. They both loved and cared for Claude as well as Shaun, their son.

Claude's family lived far away. Hence, while they supported the two partners, they were not so intimately involved in Claude's care. When Claude died they allowed Shaun to arrange the burial. Shaun purchased the headstone and told Claude's family to put on it whatever they wished. Later, the family called and told him the stone was in place and that they had written Claude's name, date of birth and death, and this: "Spouse of Shaun."

"My family has always been very important to me," said Dennis. "We're a very close family. We're kind of unique in how close we are. We're a very loving family and very demonstrative in that way." His Native American tradition found its best expression in the love his family gave him. The family of his partner, Hal, was close to Hal but not so close to Dennis. But once Hal got ill and they told his parents, Dennis found that they came to respect and like him much more as they saw how much he loved Hal and how well he took care of him when they could not since they lived far away.

Ken and Lewis lived on the west coast. Ken's family lived on the other side of the country. But Ken's brother flew to their home to attend their wedding, and "Mom was here the day before Lewis died and stayed two weeks and really helped me through a very difficult emotional time." Lewis's family was even more unusual. Ken said this about them: "They've been extraordinarily supportive. They accepted me as a member of the family right from the very beginning. His parents, both in their late seventies, are retired. His father was a highly placed officer in a very fundamentalist and conservative religious organization. Yet, there's been none of the religious bigotry that one might expect. They have taught me a great deal about tolerance and acceptance. They've accepted me as part of the family."

In their families, all these couples found support, love, and empowerment to live fully as gay couples in the context of AIDS. We can see as well that these men affected their parents deeply. The lives of the parents could never be the same once they were told of their sons' lives as gay men in love. The interaction and mutuality of parents with their sons and sons' partners in this journey created opportunities for all to grow.

The discovery that their son was gay and living with another man in a relationship as deep as their own — and perhaps even deeper — challenged the parents to look at the maturity of their own lives as well as that of their son and his lover. As they related to the partners involved in their process of living and dying, the parents came to understand more than ever what relationship is about.

Moreover, the partners found themselves empowered to live out the meaning they had found together because of the daring and support of their mothers and fathers. In such experiences we find what parenthood and lover relationship are about. Parents are to provide a context of wholeness in which children can develop — and not only dependent children, but adult ones as well. In providing a freeing love, parents empower their offspring to find or deepen the meaning which motivates every human life. Nor is it a one-way street. In deciding to live their love as a couple, partners provide the opportunity for their parents to look at themselves and their values. Seeing their son loving another man, they are often challenged to examine previously accepted norms or values. In the process they may discover how they have been influenced by society's heterosexist structures, which have oppressed their gay sons deeply.

While the parents we have just discussed were supportive, other stories I heard in my interviews moved in different directions.

Families: Some Important, Some Not

For Duncan, who had been married before his relationship with Cliff, family had great importance. His former wife and children remained close to him despite some difficulties. Duncan noted that his family not only provided support, but gave him a sense of continuity which grounded him in history — and reality. After an initial period in which he and his father were not close, they developed a relationship which meant a great deal to Duncan. Furthermore, he and his brother, who lived in the same city, were very close. Because he "always liked the idea of being a gay man with kids," he felt part of something wider than his relationship with Cliff. All these people were present in Duncan's life not just superficially but as an essential element. They contributed to a spirituality in which he found freedom to love.

Frank said, "My family is extremely important in my life. They have no idea how important they are to me." His family was his point of being rooted — a place to go, someone to call and to speak with about his life, hopes, and dreams. Because he had been shy as a child, his family "was all I ever had." He depended upon their presence, being there for him.

Neither Keith nor Sloan was close to his family. Keith said, "I don't come from a touchy-feely-huggy type of family." Sloan came from a broken family and both his mother and father lived a long distance away, which was fine with him. In their relationship Keith and Sloan found intimacy — an intimacy which they lacked in their natural family.

Stan's relationship with his family was never solidly established, "My family are fundamentalists, and I had a very difficult time growing up. I couldn't do any of the regular things that all my friends were doing. I left my family at seventeen and came to California. That was forty years ago. I go back every six or seven years. We're not close. They don't even know me. At a family reunion, we met this young girl with a baby. We didn't even know her. And she told us she was going to be praying for us guys and that we'd meet a nice girl and that everything would be all right. That's how they feel." Caught in imprisoning religious beliefs, Stan's family could not grasp or be challenged by his life which meant so much to him. Thus, they missed a chance for their own growth and development.

For Greg, his relationship with his family was stressed due to a variety of factors. As Roman Catholics to have their son become a priest was a focal point of their lives. When Greg left the priest-hood, that was bad enough, but that he entered into a relationship with another man was even more difficult for them. Greg's relation-ship with his family deteriorated after his brother's death, when Greg was unable to attend the funeral because his partner Al was dying in the hospital at the time. All these events took place over a ten-year period during which Greg attempted to maintain a dialogue with his family.

For parents in our society, it is not always easy to relate to gay sons. Social factors conspire to cause needless shame and guilt, espe-cially for those from certain religious backgrounds. However, Greg's parents attempted to work things through with his help. When we spoke, his family had reached a point where Greg could say, "It was a growing process, and I think they respect that I have a life and a ministry. They don't understand, but they're trying to respect it."

Chosen Families

Harry spoke of coming from a dysfunctional family who did not seem to understand his life or his reconnection with spirituality. When he went home for a few days at a time, he seemed to be performing a duty of some sort. His heart was not there, as he indicated when he said, "My family is not as important as my extended family."

For Harry, the Metropolitan Community Church became his cho-sen family. "The people in this church are my family plus a few friends outside the church. I have a close lesbian friend as well. They support me, and that's my family." This church has become a real home to many gay men and lesbians. For those who value Chris-tian faith, it is sometimes only here that they feel they can find an integration of their faith and their lives as gay men and lesbians. The pastor, assistants, and members of the church seek to form a community of people living in a way that incorporates all their aspi-rations of love and faith as well as their sexual orientation. For many whose former churches and families have rejected them, this church is precisely what they have been searching for.

Frank described his relationship with his own biological family in this way: "A little over seven years ago, I came out. My family is in Texas. They pretty much shunned me at that point. Nothing dra-matic, nothing spoken, just no more communication. Family, rather than my blood family, is an extended family. I have lots of extended family, caring friends who love me enough and are willing to care."

Many gay men find themselves in similar situations. As they develop deep friendships both within and outside the gay community, these friendships become the foundation for familial acceptance when their own relatives have distanced themselves. In this family they find the support they need to develop as human beings. Even those gay men whose families are understanding find friendships within the gay community extremely helpful. They realize that only other gay men and women can truly understand what it means to live as a minority in a society that has not really understood and has in fact done all it can to eliminate the possibilities for gay men and women to live fully and humanly.

Lou had both a loving family and an extended one. His parents loved him and his partner Kean very much. To Lou they were very important. "That's my blood family. I have a chosen family here as well. My chosen family is the nucleus of almost all my social activities. That's a group of six or eight people. We get together on holidays and have a cabin at the river that we go to almost every weekend in the summer. We sit at each other's houses and take care of each other's pets. So it's a very important thing." After Kean became ill and died, Lou's chosen family became even closer. "They planned special things that I didn't know about until later. Kean's voice was taped and is going to be incorporated into a tape. Another friend took pictures, and he's developing a video. They did it secretly." They had really loved the two of them and were there for him through the loss. Their presence, encouragement, and love empowered Lou to continue to live as fully as possible. Both families became constitutive elements of the couple's developing spirituality.

Families Supportive after Illness

When Jason's mother found out that he was gay, she did not want him at home. She was not ready to be face-to-face on a day-to-day basis with the gayness of her son. And certainly she was not ready to face a relationship in which her son might be involved. It was too much for both her and her husband. However, things underwent a dramatic change when Karl, Jason's lover, was in the hospital with AIDS-related diseases. Jason recalled how he was in the hospital room with Karl when the door opened and someone came in. He looked and was astounded to see his mother. "I jumped off the cot, and I ran to the door to stop her from coming in. And she just pushed her way past me. And she looked at Karl and said, 'My God, he's so sick.' And then she makes the sign of the cross and kisses him on his face — *right on his lesions.* And I'm just thinking, 'Oh, God. What is going to happen next?' And she looked at me and said, 'You love him, don't you?' And I said, 'Yes, I do.' Karl was waking up, and she asked, 'And you love him, don't you?' and he said, 'Yes, I do.' And then she took both of our hands and said, 'Well, I love you both.' And that was how I was reunited with my mom." The story is an extraordinary example of how things can happen when gay couples live their lives authentically. Their very being becomes the context for families to really look at what is important in their lives. When Jason's mother did that, she found a whole new relationship of love not only with her son, but with his lover as well.

For Karl, this was a marvelous event. When he was better, he made a special effort to get Jason to visit his family. He wanted Jason to be close to his family because he knew that he loved his parents. And because he himself knew what it was like not to have such closeness, he wanted Jason to have it.

From that point on, Jason was not alone caring for Karl. He said, "My whole family got involved in his caretaking. And so for the first time in years *we became a family again.* And that's another thing we've continued to build on." Jason felt their love and concern, not only for him, but for Karl whom they now took into their own family. His Pacific Islander background provided him with a sense of the importance of family, of being all together. When his gayness became an issue, he felt an important element of his life slipping away, and it was painful. Now, by affirming Karl and Jason's love, Jason's family reestablished that important link in his life. This became the foundation for a continuing effort to enhance their biological relationship as a family unit.

Their involvement in assisting Jason to provide Karl with good care was important not only to Karl's well-being but to Jason and Karl as a couple, for it meant that their love was affirmed by their parents' love for them. Jason noted that Karl never wanted to be alone when he was ill: "So whenever nobody else would come, my father would come and sit down." Jason felt deeply that his father's choice to be with Karl was a way of saying he was really interested in Jason's life. It meant a great deal to see his father being present in this process and indeed in their relationship.

Others, like Darin, remained closeted from their parents for a long time. Although he tried to reveal himself to them at different times, he was unable until "eventually my mother brought it up and asked,

'Are you and Emile part of the gay community?' I said 'yes.' " Emile was already ill, and then Darin's family welcomed him as part of their own family. Though illness and circumstances prevented Darin and Emile from visiting the family more than once, on that occasion Darin's parents treated them as spouses.

It is not uncommon for gay men in relationships to deny themselves the support their families might have given when HIV/AIDS entered the scene. Some parents "suspect" their son is gay, but prefer not to speak about it. Others, like Darin's, finally ask so that they can be a full part of their son's life. Other parents simply do not even think of it, perhaps subconsciously wanting it not to be true.

Steve had told his mother that he was gay in 1989, but it was such a shock that he decided he would not tell her that Sean, his partner, had AIDS. Steve was a Native Canadian and was not really close to his father. Shortly after Sean died, Steve continued the cover-up by telling his parents that Sean and he had broken up and that was why they were not together anymore. A full year passed before he told the whole story to both his parents, "When I finally told them she seemed already to know. She just didn't want to hear it at the time. Since then we've become very close. My father hugs me, which is really a big thing for me."

From that time on, he also became closer to his whole family. His fears of rejection removed, he could concentrate on deepening the relationship with his family. This affected his spirituality since the energy he had expended on secrecy could now be channelled in more positive directions. The stories he had heard about other gay men being rejected by their parents were no doubt strong reasons why he kept his identity and his relationship hidden. This is unfortunate, but not rare in the gay community. Coming out remains part of the challenge to the development of the gay man's spirituality. To grow authentically in spirituality, the masks need to be dropped — even if it takes time. The inner struggle around issues of coming out affect how and what one attempts to integrate as an ultimate value, which is central to the process of one's spirituality.

Rico found that while his family was very important to him and becoming even more so, he spent a lot of time as a "peacemaker." He was always trying to mediate and bring his discordant family together. He continued this even when he became "really pissed off because I feel I've been through a lot, and I just can't take the bullshit." When his grandmother, whom he loved very much and with whom he was very close, found out about Jon's illness, she was afraid to visit and this continued even after Jon's death. Rico said, "She didn't know that I was positive too. I didn't say it in anger, but I told her that I have it too. You could see she was looking for someone to blame so I told her I had it before. So, she's changed." Other members of his family reacted the same way, and Rico was delighted by the change in them after they knew the full story. Jon's family also supported Rico once he told them of Jon's situation. After Jon's death, one of his brothers called Rico every two or three weeks, and that made him feel respected and happy.

Partner's Families: Some Important, Some Not

While Stan did not find his own family important, he was very close to Mario's. "They treat us as we were — a couple together. His mother would come to our house twice a week. She treats me like a son. She calls me every Saturday even to this day. His family is extraordinary. I guess that's why he was so pure."[58] For Stan, the support Mario's family gave him enabled him to go through the loss of his deeply loved partner.

Chris, whose own family consisted only of two nieces, noted how incredibly important Phil's family were and are. "They are my family. They were always there for us. . . . The family has turned to me a lot for understanding Phil — why he moved here, why he was never comfortable coming out to the family. His family was incredibly important." From Phil's family Chris not only received the support he needed, especially at the time of Phil's death, but he became the source of the family members' own growth as they sought to understand their son more.

Tom spoke of the very difficult relationship he had with his own family: "Even when my mother died, my father said he would have closed the casket if he knew I was coming home. . . . My family did everything in their power to turn everyone against me because I'm gay. I've never been invited home in twenty years. I've gone home every year until three years ago — that's the last time I went . . . I've tried to maintain the bonds but I'm tired. I used to feel loved by them, but I don't believe that any longer." He tried and tried, but they refused to accept him. Denied family life, he was overwhelmed by Tim's family, who made him one of themselves. "This past Christmas was the first time in twenty years I spent Christmas with a family. They were opening presents and I was opening presents . . . It was so overwhelming I had to go upstairs and I broke down. I couldn't believe it. I'm almost fifty years old and only now experiencing a family that was happy and joyful, caring for each other and accepting me into their home to be a part of the celebration." What had been denied him so long, but what Tim's family gave him so freely, created within Tom a new energy to live fully this new stage of his life.

Frank had met Randy's family for the first time when Randy was in the hospital. "His mother came to visit. I was scared: 'Mama was coming to visit!' She got here and I fell in love with her. She's become really important. The father — we keep a little space between us, but it's a healthy space. It's okay. He's a very good and gentle man. I'm glad to have them as family." Hesitation and fear vanish with understanding given and love received.

Jack was orphaned when he was very young. With only two brothers left, he found a split in relationships. "My older brother and his wife and kids have pretty much cut off all contact with me and my partner because they believe in a fundamentalist point of view. A couple of years ago, I talked with them and told them that I hoped they would have a wonderful and joyous life and literally just said, 'This is it. If you want to speak to me that's fine and if not, that's fine too. Your life is your life and my life is mine.' My younger brother and his wife and kids and I get along famously. I'm godfather to his kids. We're Uncle Jack and Uncle Jerry. The kids come and stay with us. It's just the opposite." The younger brother and his wife knew about Jerry's diagnosis and expressed concern. "They always ask and want to know if there's anything they can do." As for Jerry's family, Jack followed Jerry's wishes not to tell his parents of his diagnosis. Though he finds it uncomfortable being silent, he does so out of respect for Jerry. "I love his father as much as I loved my own father. His mother is nice and friendly and I enjoy her company, but I really feel I have a strong relationship with his father and I feel I love him." To be in a relationship of love with parents is natural. When one's own family cannot be there, the partner's family can help fill that void and empower one to go on.

Dennis, whose own family was very close to him, found that at first Hal's mother and father needed more time. They discovered that Hal was gay just before he got seriously ill. They found it difficult to deal with, but when they saw how close Hal and Dennis were and how marvelously Dennis took care of him when he was ill, the relationship changed. "Because they were so far away they had to rely on me for caretaking...and I stuck by him. His family really respected that."

Friends as Supportive

Friendship is one of the most important elements in a life authentically lived. In our socialization as human beings, the presence or absence of friends is extremely significant. No person develops as a human being without that sense of intimacy which friendship brings into one's life. As the person grows, it is not just a question of relating to different people in a *general* way. Rather growth takes place as we relate to those with whom we develop a sense of trust flowing from a special attraction to those individuals. This is particularly the case for adolescents whose moving into adulthood is fraught with difficulties as body and spirit strain for acceptance and help. To move through this period successfully, teenagers join groups to find a sense of belonging in the turbulent, unknown land they are beginning to experience. For gay adolescents, the process can be even more fraught with danger as they come to discover their uniqueness due to their sexual orientation.

All human beings search for friendship where we can be "safe" with the other. That relationship empowers us to proceed in life with confidence that we are not alone and will not only receive support in life's difficulties, but be able to offer support to the other as friend. This special relationship is often one that seems to make life worth living. In fact, as Jason said of friends, "They're actually, I think, what gives your life meaning."

Friends as Providing Life

Several partners spoke of how important friends were as they struggled with their own seropositive status and/or that of their lovers. Duncan was one of those for whom friendship was crucial not only as he moved through caring for Cliff, but especially as he later moved through his own dying process. He said, just three months before his own death, "Friends are what make me alive. Part of the way I heal is by having people around. This place has just been full of people, bringing food, coming and taking care of things, and so forth.... I love people. They're where I get my energy." At Duncan's funeral, the homilist noted that in the past few weeks Duncan had told her that his friends who visited him provided him continuing contact with the world outside the walls of his apartment. They gave him life and provided him with meaning as he journeyed on his path. His friends knew how important it was for Duncan to have them with him, and it was important for them to have Duncan with them.

The mutuality formed their friendship and sustained them in the spiritual journey.

Friends often became sources of hope as the partners struggled with the impending loss of one who had meant so much in their lives and as they wondered how they would be able to continue, or even survive the loss. Todd noted that phone conversations and visits from friends reminded him that he was not alone, that others cared for his "well-being as well as the health of your friend." Greg said, "Friends are absolutely important. They are family. I think, for me, friends were a vital part of the whole process of sustaining me and Al through HIV and the illnesses. And they were also very instrumental for the healing process in myself. They were there for me. They listened. They encouraged. They celebrated.... And they are part of the healing process and they continue to be." He spoke of the closest friends whose constant support enabled him to go on both during Al's illness and after his death. Others, he noted, became more distant. "That's because of some of the issues revolving around HIV and the gay community, which at times wants to party and deny the status of HIV." As we will see with other stories, in the context of HIV/AIDS, some friendships can wither while new ones can develop.

In all this, the presence of friends removes an isolation which could easily destroy the caregiving partner. Frank said it well: "I believe staunchly that we are not meant to be alone. We're supposed to share life. Isolation is probably the tragedy because when there's isolation, there's hopelessness. The real gift for me is the sharing." Because of the support of his friends, Frank found that he was able to be more available to other people, so that they could come to talk with him and he with them.

Jack found that his friends validated him for who he was. "They remind me of things that have happened to me and of how my life has evolved and changed. And I like them and enjoy their company. We're able to talk about things.... They are people I can rely on." To have someone we can communicate with openly empowers us to see the whole persons we are becoming. The presence of such friends becomes part of our life process, without which we might not have had the opportunity to develop the potential which lies within. Like some others, Jack was not concerned that his friends would change if they discovered that his partner had AIDS. Their bond was too strong to be destroyed by this ravaging disease.

After Bobby's death, Harry could say, "I'd rather have a close friend than a lover. What's a friend? Someone you can rely on. You can rely on friends for support, to be a pain in the butt. My friends can make me laugh. I have people I've grown to love as friends. That wasn't always true in my life. The more I belong, the more I appreciate the diversity of people. I have so many friends now. They all play different roles. With some it's just saying 'Hello' every Sunday. . . . Friends make my life very rich in a way that it wasn't before. I didn't have it living in an isolated little place. Now it's a constant wellspring. I can't expect any better — well, maybe if I had a lover." From such diverse relationships develops an appreciation for the variations in life. Friends break us out of our self-imposed exile and in loving us challenge us to see the beauty which surrounds us.

In any context, friends become such an intimate part of our life that we do not have to hide anything from them or put on airs. For Rick and Phil, close friends meant "people who will stand by you through thick and thin. They know what is going on. . . . Our friends worry about our health and that we take care of each other. They're great people. I'd go to the wall for them, and I know they'd do the same for me. . . . We'll argue in front of them. Like the last time Phil said, 'You don't understand anything. You don't know what it's like to be HIV positive.' Our friend was there. That's when I lit into him." Friendship creates a mutuality where people not only receive but give and are concerned about the other. Friends provide a safe space where people can be fully themselves without fear of being rejected. Rick said, "I really worry about the impact of Phil's getting worse on them. But in terms of whether they would still be there — that's not a problem. I know these people. They're terrific. My concern would not be that they would take off. It would be the impact on them and that they would be devastated." The mutuality which is of the essence of true friendship provides one's friends with the support and space to live out an experience of pain and loss.

Only a Few Friends

In the North American context, some people living with HIV/AIDS find that their circle of friends is limited. Keith and Sloan's best friends were a straight couple, whose female partner was particularly close to Sloan. "But gaywise, I've outlived all of mine, or the ones we did have were bar friends. When we became a couple they just sort of dropped us. So we really don't have friends." Stan described a similar situation: "Well, friends are very important, but I don't have many left. In the city I have about four friends left. I used to have forty. They're all dead. I've got one real good friend

I've known for twenty-some years, and he's real sick now.... All the friends who could help me in the turmoil I'm going through are not here anymore. It disturbs me because I can't seem to meet friends. I used to have so many friends and now..."

Keith and Stan noted two limitations to friendship in the gay male community. The first, which both experienced, is the devastating impact of HIV/AIDS upon the community.[59] Thousands have died, ravaged by this horrible disease. It has left the survivors alone in many cases, often searching for friends for consolation. Others have simply given up this search for fear that the disease will take from them yet more of those to whom they have become close. Living through this time of sickness and death inevitably affects one's spirituality.

The second element has to do with the coupled relationship of many gay men. When they enter into such a relationship their single friends may drift away. Or the couple itself may move away from their previous activities, such as visiting the bars or other places where they established friendship with other gay men. They may limit their relationships to other couples. Jake noted, "Usually what happens when I get in a relationship is that my lover becomes my best friend and usually my other friends will say, 'You must have a lover. I don't hear from you any more.'" As a result, when one's partner falls ill or dies, one is left without friends and one may feel he is too old to try to establish other friendships in the usual places. Unfortunately, there are few places other than bars where gay men can meet and develop healthy friendships, though in San Francisco and other places people are trying to organize groups and activities where such friendships can develop.

Jake also noted how HIV/AIDS affected his own sense of belonging. "Another friend, John, was also positive. So I felt there were certain issues I could talk to John about, but there were other issues I felt I couldn't talk about.... There was a whole group of people that Ricky was sick with who were my friends as well. We sort of bonded together, but I also felt very much like an outsider in that group." Being the partner of one who lives with HIV/AIDS can open new doors of sharing, but it can also create an atmosphere where the seronegative person feels left out.[60]

Chris found that friends were important, but he added, "it's a difficult area. I find it interesting that I don't have any friends here who are men and who are gay. I've lived here for twelve years. There are men here who are gay, but I don't classify them as good friends. My

three closest friends are women who are heterosexual." When Chris
established friendships, he did so intending them to last. Since he had
lived in other places, his friends were spread out over the country. As
a result he lacked the continuous contact which would have helped
him when his lover was ill and dying.

When Tom and Tim had problems, Tom could talk to a friend
over lunch. As Tom put it, he was the "only outlet I had." While he
did have other friends with whom he could open up, it was not the
same. With all these partners, there were at least a few people whom
they considered as friends. Others, however, did not have any friends
at all — either by choice or circumstance.

Independence, Distance, and Friends

While Frank saw his family as very important, friendship seemed to
have a negative impact on him in the HIV/AIDS context. "I didn't
care much for friends because I've always taken care of myself," he
said. "I had a friend; that friend found out that my partner was positive. I don't have that friend anymore. It did bother me because this
was the only friend I ever had since I was a kid. But because of that
I never heard from him again. Today, as far as friends are concerned,
I don't look for friends." Frank found his brothers and sisters to be
friends, though his relationship with his mother was a bit strained
because of her inability to face the fact that he had a lover. "When
I would see her, my mother would say, 'Those people you're taking care of, how are they?' I would think to myself, 'These people
I'm taking care of? This is my lover!' And then I would say, 'Oh,
we're doing fine, mother.'" She tried to be interested, but the relationship seemed too much for her. Not to have that affirmation
bothered Frank, even as he tried to understand.

Darin had a limited circle of friends because of a variety of
circumstances. He said, "I've always thought I've been alone and independent in life, sort of finding my way without my family as far as
being a gay person and things, making decisions about the future and
my lifestyle. But I think in losing Emile in the past year, I've come to
see that friends are important. My best friend was Emile. My friends
are more important than my family." As for many gay men, Darin's
being gay hindered a deeper relationship with his family. As a result,
he had moved away — physically — and lived his own life, ultimately
facing and accepting who he was. Finding Emile, he surrendered his
total independence and found how important friends were in his life.

Steve had been on his own since he was sixteen. "I've always been a very independent person and I thrived on that. . . . I cut off a lot of friends when I was a teenager. When I was younger, I didn't really have a lot of friends either, because of my family. And I didn't want to bring friends over. But now I see how much support I could get from friends and how much they really cared — cards and letters when Sean died." Like Darin, Steve had tried to be totally independent. The terrible loss he suffered when Sean died after eight years of a relationship became the turning point with regard to his ideas about friendship. This was important since he himself was HIV positive and needed a wider community which could empower him to live fully. He and Sean had kept their diagnoses a secret from their friends for a time. When they found out, the friends wanted to be closer and "they told me after that that they were upset that we didn't tell anybody. At the funeral, I thought there'd be only a couple of people there, but it was packed. It helped me get through that day."

Karl and Thomas lived in a rural area, without much opportunity to find and nurture friendships. The friends they had made earlier in their lives lived either in other countries or distant states. Thomas's sickness and death, said Karl, "sorted out some friendships for me. Some became remarkably close, and I feel a great deal of appreciation toward certain people. And other people just drifted away and that was probably the best thing." They had chosen to tell those closest to them about their HIV situation; others they did not tell because they did not expect these would understand. "Some of those, it was surprising because they wished I had said something. But I didn't trust them and I wish I had." Having denied himself such support, Karl found that after Thomas died, he needed it. "It was our battle when he was alive, but afterward I had my own struggle, and that's when the lack of support really hurt. I didn't want or really need people helping with things. He was able to do quite a lot for somebody who was weakened so much. But afterward, after the death, there was this huge vacant open space of the house and I still had the same responsibilities. The transition for me was terrible, maybe because I didn't have those contacts right where I was living. I wish I did have." As Karl found, community is essential to living in a whole, healthy way. When our fears keep us from tapping into the resources of the community, we suffer. Suffering can never be totally removed, but it can be made more bearable because of the friends we have.

Jess and Max had been very closeted. When Max fell ill, Jess had no one to talk to because Max did not want anyone in their city to know. Jess had only his brother, who lived far away. Fortunately, the brother put him in contact with someone who was part of an AIDS committee in another city. These two contacts helped Jess with his "emotional coping." Eventually, he contacted the AIDS committee in his own city. He reached out for help because "I felt I needed more support during the time that Max was sick, but probably more so when he died and I felt alone." Not having been part of the gay community, HIV/AIDS isolated them terribly. When Jess saw that he needed help, he finally decided to break out of the closet. His and Max's suffering and his ultimate reaching out to people became important elements of his spirituality. In fact, the support Jess finally received gave him new insight into an authentic spirituality.

Having come from another region of Canada, Ronald had only one friend in his city, are with whom he had studied. His friend was straight, but accepting of gay people. When Ronald told him of Kerry's illness, "he accepted it. I can count on his help. He is a person who is devoted, devoted to his friends. His friends can count on him, and he can always count on me." Though his friendships were limited, Ronald realized how fortunate he was to have one person with whom he could share and in whom he could find support. Moreover, his commitment to his friend demonstrated the mutuality which must be a part of any real friendship.

Religion and Spiritual Beliefs

If family and friends are essential elements in human life, one would also think that religion with its strong social dimension would provide support for the partners. The founders of all major religions intended to provide a path which would enhance human life in its varied circumstances. Ideally, religion provides community and direction to empower people to find meaning in life. Religious beliefs underlie many persons' values, choices, goals, and relationships. Their impact may be subtle, unconscious, or overt. At times it may seem as if a person has no spiritual system out of which to function, yet a traumatic experience may reveal deeply rooted beliefs which seemed absent. Other times, when such beliefs seem evident, a tragic event may reveal their superficiality. Whether deep or superficial, one's beliefs may or may not be connected to an organized religion. In what follows, we shall examine the role religion and spiritual beliefs play in the lives of those partners living with HIV/AIDS.

Absence of Spiritual or Religious Beliefs

Despite or perhaps because of being raised within a strict Roman Catholic tradition, Jason at first claimed that he did not have any religious beliefs which provided him with support. Yet, as he continued to speak he revealed that this might not be the case. "I learned to talk to God. And I trained as a rebirther. I read all these New Age books.... It's like I reawakened a spirituality in me. I guess HIV and AIDS have done that." At one time while Karl was still alive, "I was writing a letter to God and asking him if he might spare Karl. I said that in my lifetime I know that I've turned my back. I was raised a very strict Catholic, and just maybe I've not been the best person. But I asked him if there was anything that he could do. If there was, it should be done now, or, if he couldn't answer that prayer, I would understand. But if there was one thing he could do, if he could be merciful and spare him." Despite Jason's conscious attitudes about religion, a relationship with God remained and provided him with a presence he deemed important. Jason discovered in that relationship himself and his path and affirmed that God was an intimate part of the love which he and Karl shared.

Religion, however, provided no supportive role for him. He said so clearly, adding, "I guess for me, the higher power is God and that is who I talk to. I put my faith in the universe and things, but basically it's God." In this statement, Jason revealed his connection with the whole of creation — a connection found in everything he said in his interview. This connection had existed in him since his childhood in the Pacific, where nature was as an important element in the Islanders' worldview. Jason's ancestral spiritual belief system grounded him in nature and life.

Frank felt comfortable being an agnostic. He maintained he did not have religious or spiritual beliefs. About religion he said, "It's something I have a very hard time believing in. I know that when hard times are there I will say, 'God help me.' I do that like everybody else. Whether I believe that or not, I don't know." After Fabian died, he made "a conscious attempt to want to believe in God as before I would not." Having identified religion and God, he could not believe before this. Now he was able to separate God from religion up to a point, though not completely. Belief still demanded an attempt to will an experience repugnant to him. Yet, underlying all, one sees in Frank's devotion to Fabian a belief system that was indeed present and helpful even when not articulated. While Fabian was ill, Frank found religion supportive for Fabian. "If there isn't a heaven, he's creating one. That's how much he believed it. So I found it supportive for him. I also found it supportive for me in a way. He believed so much in it that I knew when he died, whether it's there or not, he's going to go there. There was no doubt in his mind that he was going to go there. That was a form of support." It was in Fabian's spiritual belief system that Frank found a foundation for his effort to believe. This was not a belief in religion as such, but a belief in a life beyond death — a life related to God. Their relationship had a positive impact on Frank, demonstrating how we grow in our interaction with people, especially those we love and who love us.

Rico noted that he had always claimed to be a "somewhat" spiritual person. However, at the time that Jon was ill, he did not seem to be drawing on any spiritual beliefs. He said, "At that time no. I didn't see it. I was on automatic pilot. I wasn't seeing anything, and I didn't have time for anything. I used to say I believed in God, but I wasn't sure I really believed in God." Though both he and Jon had been raised Catholic, he did not find this religion supportive. "I have a problem with the Catholic Church. I don't go to church at all." Jon's sister had sent Rico a note saying, "I'd really appreciate it if you had a priest come in and do a prayer for the sick. Have a prayer for the sick. You know priests are very forgiving of your lifestyle." Because of the request and because he thought that Jon might want it, he called a priest. Though the priest came, Rico felt "it was terrible. My lover was dying, and this priest was just doing his thing." He found no support there. The priest's mechanical actions reinforced Rico's judgment that the church could offer him little support. Then, after Jon's death, Rico found himself in a dramatic state: "I wanted to kill myself after he died. I thought of that every day, every day for weeks. Finally, I found a place where I could do it, but by then . . . something inside me . . . Then I went through a stage where I felt, 'I don't care if I live or die.' I started asking God for strength and saying, 'If I'm meant to be here, let me find happiness in life or something; and sure enough, I can laugh now. I don't think these are things we create ourselves, but sometimes I still cry a lot. Looking at his picture or listening to some music I'll be crying and I'm feeling such joy at the same time. That has to be something higher than myself. And I feel like I'm receiving energy and sending it back. I think that's Jon too." What previously had been words became reality. Rico's spiritual belief system affirmed God's presence and his continued connection with Jon, who had gone before him. With this, life became worth living once more. However, religion was not part of this new life.

While he felt that he did not have any spiritual or religious beliefs to help him deal with his partner's diagnosis, Keith had some spiritual foundations. "Probably most of my spiritual strength comes from inside and from Native American–type spirituality. And that's just developed since we've come together. I wasn't an atheist, but I saw religion as a farce." Like so many gay men, Keith had "some really bad experiences with organized religion," and they led him to reject institutional religion. And though he would quickly and firmly deny anything "spiritual" connected with religion, his relationship with Sloan, whose theological training affected their relationship, opened new doors to the spiritual dimension of being human. Within each of us lies that which seeks deeper meaning, and various events in our day-to-day lives touch that level. With a certain openness, what lies within becomes free to express itself as we examine and live it more fully. Native American openness to another world within this world empowered Keith to tap those depths, while other religious traditions left him without any positive feelings.

While Todd maintained that he had no beliefs which helped him during Denny's illness and death, his deep love for Denny told another story. Todd was a paraplegic when they had met. They lived together for seven years before Denny's death. Todd clearly gained strength from his belief in their love. It was this that enabled him to care for Denny at home until just a few months before Denny's death. From his wheelchair, he would feed, bathe, and take care of Denny and even carry him to the car to take him to the doctor. But one day, when Denny had fallen on the floor and Todd could not pick him up, he realized that he had to bring him to the hospice where he could be cared for. It was a difficult decision for him to make, as he wanted to take care of Denny himself. Denny had been a Catholic, and eight days before he died, Todd called a priest to come to offer the sacrament of the sick. This religious event "gave me satisfaction that the way for him is being made so that when the time comes he will go to the better place than what he has now." With his spiritual openness and love, Todd found some help in a religious belief which was not his own.

Presence of Spiritual or Religious Beliefs

For Duncan, spiritual beliefs were essential. "My spirituality has to do with trusting God and God's grace and God's wisdom, which means I've had to deepen that. And so, I've had to really trust it, learn to trust it — even more." To understand that God loved and was part of all life became essential to Duncan's life and his life with Cliff. For Duncan God was not some dogma, but a living reality, a reality that he wanted to become the core of his life. He found he was in a constant process of coming to trust even more. Every event in life challenged or enlivened that trust. Life for Duncan was an interaction with a God who loved and lived with him.

It was religion and life that brought him to see this. Duncan found the supportive element of religion in the parish he went to "and other parts of the Episcopal Church." Religion was not simply an institution for him. It was also people who enhanced his life. It was individuals who tried to live the path of love in relationship with him. During Cliff's illness and in his death, Duncan found that his beliefs changed in the sense that they deepened. "I went through a couple of periods where I got very manipulative in my spirituality and realized I was trying to fend off death and everything else — and laughed eventually when I realized what I was doing. So I realized that things deepened and you go through periods where you have to try on something new, and if it doesn't work, it doesn't work. And it didn't. So, I came back to who I was in my relationship with God."

It was only when Emile died that Darin discovered what his own beliefs had been. "I guess I had a faith that things would work out and would be fine, because when he did die it pulled the rug out. I had never had a clue that that day would come." After Emile's death, "I've done a lot of soul searching this year — spiritual issues. I haven't completely figured all that out yet but I'm a lot closer than I was then. I think I was so busy living it that I didn't have time to meditate on it. I've done more meditation and thinking since then." When someone we love is ill and dying, the whole of our consciousness focuses on him. In order to get through it, we sometimes try to convince ourselves that ultimately everything will be fine. Maybe this medicine will work, or that treatment will conquer it. Then there is the minute-by-minute care that is required. He's not eating. What would he like? Trips to the store to get it. How can I help him in his pain? What should I do next? Laundry load after laundry load. Cleaning up after him. How can I go on? Thousands of questions and things to do. Each caregiver experiences such things in his own way. Darin found that his belief or hope that all would be fine enabled him to do what needed to be done for Emile. But Emile's death made it all come crashing down. The challenge to Darin became to see where these events had brought him and how he could live more fully the moment in which he found himself.

Being a theologian by profession, Sloan had already been dealing with AIDS and theology in his work. As he said, however, "Having to deal with it among friends meant I couldn't just give easy answers around the issues. I'm not sure that the HIV stuff affected the theological position or vice versa." As with everything else in theology, when something touches one's person and relationships, it affects one's thought processes. In Sloan's case, this "something" was meeting Keith and becoming involved with him. As Sloan said, he now could not give easy answers to hard questions. Sloan had to struggle through the ups and downs of HIV because it was very much a part of their life together. As far as religion goes, Sloan concluded that "I don't find institutional religion helpful at all."

Tim was alive when I interviewed Tom, who said, "Every day is a spiritual day if he's alive. There are too many times when I feel I can't do anything. I can't make it better. When we go to church (it's not often anymore), I feel God has allowed us to spend our life together in a better way. We need to thank God that we're together and that we are here now when a year and a half ago he almost died. When he tells me about the difference I've made in his life and that I've got him through things, I feel God is present in our lives. I'm a firm believer in God and in his power or its power." In the face of Tim's illness, Tom's helplessness was assuaged by the gift of their relationship — a gift which he felt came from God. This made him realize the wonder of God's presence in their life together. This belief in God underlay everything for Tom and empowered him to live out every moment he and Tim shared. God was not *out there* somewhere, but very much alive *in* their relationship. When asked whether religion was important to him, Tom responded saying, "I'm finding some religious themes — poetry, reading, life after death, and the thought that he'll be waiting for me on the other side. I never thought much about these things before. Because of him I now know. Thoughts about God made me believe it's possible for us to be together after death." Though they attended the Metropolitan Community only occasionally in the last year or so before Tim died, religion clearly meant more than just an institution to them. Tom lived in his faith in God.

Ken had a similar attitude. While he did some work in both the United Church of Christ and the Metropolitan Community Church, he strongly believed that God's presence was to be found in people. This belief formed the foundation for how he dealt with Lewis's illness. "I guess my belief is that God is present in those who gather around us. Around eighteen or twenty people gathered to support us — volunteers, medical staff, hospice staff, colleagues, other ministers, those who came to pray with us. They all manifested God's presence and created the sense of the Holy Spirit in our lives." In these experiences the life of God in the Spirit became embodied and deeply human for Ken. God cared. God touched. God loved in the people who surrounded them. This enfleshed God did not stand aloof from the sorrows and joys of human life, but rather was intimately involved in a loving way with them.

Stan also found God in life. He spoke of his conflicts with religion and of his liberation to discover God everywhere. "I always have been conflicted with religion because of my family. Everybody else was wrong and they were right in this little church they were involved in. They didn't like the Catholics. They didn't even like other Protestant groups. We weren't allowed to have friends outside this narrow little group. I always thought about God in much broader terms than they talked about. I didn't know at the time that I was rebelling against them when I was younger. Later it was to get out of that little cocoon. I think faith did it — it helped me tremendously. But it was maybe not a faith found in any particular church. It was something I experienced in life." Institutional religions can and do work against their principal purpose. Out of a need for security some people can use institutional religion to move into a comfortable isolation. They reject anyone or anything that does not fit their particular thought pattern.

Spirituality cannot develop in such a stifling atmosphere. Authentic spirituality is all-inclusive and needs openness and a daring to risk in order to be life-giving. Stan innately realized this. He moved out of his church's closedness to find a God connected to his life, a God who sustained him. Stan understood that God cannot be contained within a little box of dogmatism or institutional beliefs.

Lou's spiritual beliefs remained constant during and after Kean's illness and death. "I think I reaffirmed what I believed. I have a story to tell you — you can make of it what you will. When Kean's mother died — he was very close to her — he went walking into the park beside our house. There was a robin, and he's always been partial to robins. He thought this robin was bringing some source and spirituality to his life. After he died, about four to five weeks after, I was at our cabin in a wooded resort area. I had never really had a chance to say goodbye to him. It was that fast. I was really grieving, and I was out walking the dogs at 5:30 in the morning. I rounded the corner, and there was a robin right in the middle of the road. The big dog who loves to chase everything was off her leash. But she stopped, wagged her tail, and did not chase the robin though it was very close to her. I thought to myself, 'Hello, Kean,' and I got a chance to say my goodbye to him through the robin and then it flew away. I think this was something very spiritual — something from God. It was a gift. It was something I needed. I think God works through ways like this if we open our eyes. I'm convinced there is a continuation of life, and it may not be as I thought it was, but there is something." If one believes in a loving God, one can feel God's touches in a variety of ways. Lou's interpretation of his encounter with the robin suggests this. It reveals as well how his belief provided him with what he needed as he journeyed in love with Kean. It was not directly connected with religion, but it was a faith which sustained him.

Greg often spoke about the Spiritual Exercises of St. Ignatius of Loyola as being important in his life. But other beliefs also came into play. "I think religion is born from the experience of wrestling with death. I was a teaching fellow for a course on comparative conceptions of the afterlife. I've dealt with a lot of death literature and interviewed people who had near-death experiences. That gave me encouragement about life, as did the experience of dealing with people who were HIV positive and who had faith — watching the progression of faith in their lives." Greg's professional and personal experience provided him with a sense of life, precisely through looking at death. It was not just an intellectual experience, though reflection was necessarily involved, but it was an embodied reality that gave him a sense of life being worthwhile. He found meaning in facing death with all the anguish that is involved. In his relationships with people, even the people whose concepts of death and life he had only read about, Greg discovered a help in the path that he and Al entered in their relationship and, ultimately, in facing Al's death.

Listening to life opens us up to meaning which we may not even have expected. This listening is very much a part of spirituality. Yet, for Greg as for many others, institutional religion offered little support as he went through Al's illness. "The institutional church for the most part is bankrupt on this issue," he said. Nevertheless, he affirmed that priest friends were supportive. This seems to be a constant in the lives of partners: while there is a clear notion that institutional religion is nonsupportive, people who are part of and represent that institution often are supportive.

Dave maintained, "I guess I had the feeling that someone was looking out for me. I had been very promiscuous, and so many people I did have sex with have died with AIDS." Though he had a Jewish background, Dave did not find Judaism of support. Whatever or whoever it was, he sensed there was a protective presence and that his life must therefore have meaning. Jack, on the other hand, had a firm belief in a God who loved people, though he rejected his early Catholic religion. "My whole Catholic upbringing is out the door because that doesn't prepare you spiritually or religiously.... My belief is that everything is in perfect order. God does it that way and has set it in motion. It's not like it's predestined...it's kind of hard to articulate. Everything will turn out the way it will turn out, whether it's good or bad. I have no say-so in that. The only thing I have is the reaction to the way things are. I guess that's where my power comes in, in the way I react to the way things are. Maybe 'power' is not the right word; maybe 'spirituality' is the better word. It's a very strong belief that God is watching over us and that nothing happens without his say-so, nod, or whatever. He's not a vengeful God (as the Catholics taught me). He's just there and it will be exactly right." Life happens in the living of it; we create our path. Over and indeed within it, God remains loving and there to help each person through the more difficult times as well as the good ones. Jack believed in a God who never desires destruction but only humanity's progressive, holistic living. With such foundational beliefs life becomes an engagement in spirituality. Jack expressed this as he spoke of religion. "I don't think the Catholic Church is that supportive, but I have found MCC supportive. Their doctrine of including everybody rather than having to pass a test to get in really appeals to me. It fits with my beliefs. In [another city], when we were going to MCC, it was a small congregation. So we became close. You knew everybody in the church and we were the church. It was nice to have people around who said, 'We love you for who you are.' There was an inclusive love. It's a little different in this larger congregation. We found you have to reach out and introduce yourself and meet people. You get out of it what you put into it. That goes back to life being a series of opportunities, and you've got to go for it. One of the ways to go for it in a new situation — a city or a congregation — is to go out there and stick your hand out and meet people. And if you don't like what's going on, then get involved in something else." Support is the affirmation of one's being. Knowing and loving others authentically takes place only when we affirm the loved ones in their totality — not as we want them to be, but as they are. Jack experienced this in his congregation and made it central to his lifestyle.

Raised as a Catholic, Dennis felt he had faith. He prayed for strength and guidance, as he put it. This provided him with help in dealing with Hal's illness. His beliefs strengthened as a result of his experience with Hal's death. He found religion supportive only in the sense that people are what makes religion. "The most supportive of the clergy was a woman from the Anglican Church that I met at the hospital when Hal was first diagnosed. She moved to Toronto, and I lost contact with her. She was incredible in helping me. She was wonderful." Being a Native American, Dennis looked to Native spirituality for help. He stayed away from the Catholic Church "because of their stand on homosexuality." It did not help either when Hal wanted to go to confession and receive communion and Dennis tried to get a priest to come. The priest he approached turned out to be "very nontolerant of the entire lifestyle and he told me that it was a condemnation from God." Dennis learned through this to move toward people who were life-giving. Whether these had official status made little difference to him. It was those who saw beyond restrictive dogmatism whom Dennis found empowering. They are the ones who feed authentic spirituality in the people they meet. They are concerned not with compliance to external rules but with living life. Dennis saw this and followed such a path.

Steve had a similar background. "I grew up as a Roman Catholic and really feel I tried to follow the rules a lot, but being gay was one of the big no-no's and that really felt hypocritical to me. And then I started to learn about Native culture and religion. I don't know if you'd call it religion — their way of the spirits. It's so down to earth and that helped a lot." He found much comfort in his Native roots. "Native culture doesn't believe in hell. The things that they preach are more earthy. It wasn't like you had to be perfect. That helped a lot." He began telling Sean about what he had found. At that time, Sean believed in nothing — death was death, the end. "That hurt me a lot because I needed something to hang on to. But in the end he had a change of attitude." While his Native beliefs gave him lots of support, Steve's encounter with Catholicism was the opposite. He spoke of a friend who went to church every day and one time told the priest that he was gay. The priest's attitude and words were very condemnatory. "When that happened I said I didn't want anything to do with the church anymore." He added that his friend then went to an Anglican church where they accepted gays and "that was a kind of relief for me, thinking that at least there is someplace that is going to accept us." Nonetheless, Steve found his real support in his Native roots.

For Cyril, belief in Jesus Christ and in "life after life" provided the support he needed to face Louis's illness and death. This did not mean that there were no problems. "Some days I lose hope, but for some reason it always comes back stronger. If I do lose hope and if I do lose touch with my faith, when I take time to meditate or pray there will always be comfort. I will feel better." He found religion supportive, but again, the support he received was not from the institution per se, but from particular priests and church members who offered love. When his mother had found out Cyril was gay, she had gone to her priest, and he told her, "It's a reason to love him more." This priest presided at Louis's funeral, and Cyril found comfort in the priest's words and in the priest's listening not only respectfully, but lovingly. Cyril also spoke lovingly of a nun who loved her "guys" as she called them and who had helped him very much. With such "religious" he found what he needed to live his faith in God authentically — even if the institution itself was not really a part of his life.

The beliefs which offered Rick support and hope as he cared for Phil came from scripture. "I guess my faith is what I believe to be expressed in John 3:16 ['For God so loved the world that he gave his only son so that whoever believed in him would not be lost but would have eternal life']. I know that seems almost evangelical. I believe in biblical Christianity. I believe in God and that he is an infinitely loving and infinitely lovely being. That doesn't mean that if you make a mistake you get hit on the side of the head — the hell fire and damnation kind of thing. I don't believe that's what God is really about. To be honest, I've actually heard that in the States there's a sticker which said, 'Kill a queer for Christ.' Anyone who can say such a thing about another person is not a Christian. I do have a strong faith, and I believe in a personal God. I don't believe I need to go to a priest to get me in touch with God." Rick had discovered the real God of Christianity, who transcends what institutions might say. This God of love formed the core of his life journey. About religion in an organized sense, he said, "I don't know if I'd use the word 'religion.' I find organized religion has a lot of hypocrisy and prejudice associated with it, whether Catholic, Anglican, or Jewish. There is a lot of built-in prejudice in all religions. I don't have much use for that. I think we all have our prejudices, but I try to overcome them. I'm not trying to make myself sound better than anyone else. I believe in biblical Christianity. I do have problems with some of the statements about homosexuality, and I don't know how biblical scholars or even evangelical Christians can reconcile what we're finding out about homosexuality now (that it's not a choice) and some of what is in the Bible. Some of what is in the Bible is social ignorance." He had attended a Free Methodist church, but found that this was not helpful to him. It was his faith in the God he found through the Bible that provided Rick what he needed to live as a gay man.

Harry's partner Bobby was a Native American who, though raised Christian, identified more with his Native roots. Harry never lost his Christian beliefs, "but I never found a place to share them or to experience them with other people.... I've always had a peace regardless of whatever was in my life. Once you've grown to love God that never goes away regardless of your life. That's what this church [MCC] is about. It's about a bunch of people who love God and didn't have anywhere to go. That's what's going to happen to Christianity in this century. They're going to have to face down this issue of gay people or they won't survive. It's too essential." Bobby's memorial service was a Catholic one, at which Harry gave a eulogy about the struggle of AIDS being like Jacob's struggle with the angel. Harry said, "I will not let thee go until thou bless me." Harry's relationship was with God, and organized religion was not an absolutely essential part of that.

– ◆ –

While society as a whole oppresses gay men with its structures and attitudes and thus has a negative impact upon their spirituality, the partners we have seen found their own way to manage their lives. Despite the added difficulties HIV/AIDS brought into their relationships, they not only managed, but enhanced their lives as they encountered various impasses. They became occasions to listen, to question, to search, and ultimately to choose to live every moment as it arose. In this choice, they uncovered ever-more involving depths of meaning, love, and hope in situations which often seemed devoid of these. We have seen the variety of reactions their biological families exhibited and how each partner found ways, sometimes with great difficulty, to integrate the elements of life in a healthy process of discovering meaning. For some, their biological families remained constant in their support as their gay sons lived lives of love with infected partners. Each family acted in its own particular way so that their sons discovered a freedom to care for their partners as the partners moved into different unambiguously painful stages of living with HIV/AIDS. The attitudes and actions of the families affected not only the spiritualities of their sons but of the new sons they were given in these gay partnerships. Though constant affirmation of sons and their partners may not be widespread, when it does occur it illustrates that it is not only possible, but desirable and necessary, if human society is to achieve its full humanity. The impact these gay men and their supportive parents have had on a limited part of society changes society as a whole little by little, whether we see this clearly or not.

But this is not the whole story. As we have seen, other families moved toward acceptance and affirmation much more slowly, and sometimes not at all. When they discovered their son's gayness or his love for another man living with HIV/AIDS, some could not put aside the strong influence of the civil and religious societies in which they lived. Some found their anger so strong that their first reaction was to reject their son.

In some of these cases, the parents' instinctive love led them to see how special their son and his partner were. Daring to cast aside the hatred of gay people which various structures of society inbred in them, they moved out to say yes to love and to their sons. Sometimes, the initial reactions of rejection led their sons to a freedom they had not known before. When an authentic relationship with their families, which most desired, was denied them, they chose to move on without the support they could normally have expected. This became an occasion to be fully who they were as gay men in love and take on the struggle to live their values. Their spirituality elicited an ever-spiraling wholeness which provided them with meaning and joy in life despite the destructiveness of HIV/AIDS.

We saw how some parents and siblings absolutely refused to accept their gay sons and their partners as anything but hateful. Though their attitudes reflected predominant societal outlooks, for the most part these people rejected and even hated their gay offspring because of a religious formation which would brook no questions about their fundamentalist interpretations of the Bible or some other radically conservative religious belief system. Caught in a dire need for absolute security and control, as were the religions to which they adhered, these parents maintained their imprisonment despite the cost to them and to their sons. As we read of their attitudes, we cannot help wondering how religion, especially one based totally upon love as Christianity is, could result in one of the most unnatural actions of a parent — the rejection of their own flesh.

Yet, even with this horrendous rejection, which no doubt was supported by factors other than religion, the sons refused to limit their growth and their lives. Difficult as it was to leave their families behind, they moved on and found new meaning in their lives, especially through the constant support of their families of choice. These friends became the means of renewed hope and meaning. Some were gay, some straight. Together they formed a safe place to be who one is and to grow into the person one is becoming. For what is a family if not that — a place where we are always loved and protected from what could harm our development? A family of choice becomes a model for biological families in the time of HIV/AIDS. For mutuality forms the very marrow of the extended family, something which all biological families should have as their prime motivating factor, but sometimes lack.

The gay partners who shared their story revealed as well the impact friends had on their lives. For most, friends were absolutely essential as they lived through the difficult time of loving a man with HIV/AIDS. It was the mutuality of friendship which empowered them to live. Friendship became the key element in life, as some became so isolated through the fear of disclosure, and others found that friends drifted away when they discovered that one or both of the partners lived with HIV/AIDS.

Still others found themselves with no friends, or hardly any, since all had already died from AIDS. Living at a distance also left some partners without the support of long-lasting friendship. All of these, whether they had the close support of friends, or whether they discovered only after the death of their lover how important friends were, found through these relationships that life and death could have meaning. This enabled them to continue the process, assured that they would grow spiritually and psychologically to make a difference in the world.

And finally, religion and spirituality found their places in a variety of ways in the stories we have heard. Almost all the partners had long before left their religion of origin. As with most gay men, the partners found these institutions had created such conflict within them as they struggled with being gay that they could no longer remain in these prisons of torture and guilt. Sometimes they identified institutional religion with God or spirituality and believed they had to reject those as well. Some thought they had no spiritual or religious belief system to empower them to live the experience of AIDS with their partner.

Yet, as they spoke, it became evident that they lived out of a positive spirituality that provided them with hope. For others, the belief system developed after the death of the one they loved. Others maintained a deep spiritual belief that often included a sense of the presence of God, and this was what enabled them to live the experience as fully as possible. Native systems of belief provided others with a sense of connection with the earth and with life and death. This afforded hope that death did not mean the end of their love. While most, if not all, rejected institutional religion, some found that individuals such as priests, nuns, or pastors were sacraments of God in their lives. These people helped them to find the courage to go on despite the ever-present threat of loss and destruction.

All these stories reveal how we are all connected. We cannot hear them without realizing that we are not alone. Contained within this realization is another: that people and the earth itself provide every person the possibility to live fully and face the questions of suffering and death. We might not find a concrete answer to these questions other than that everything is to be lived as consciously as possible; and we can do that only if others are there with us in the process. Here is the very heart of community and what it means to live in the presence of the sacred.

Chapter 6

Images of God and Prayer

As we grow up we encounter various images of God, some of which anchor us in life. Churches, synagogues, and Native traditions speak to us of a transcendent power that is related and connected to us. Sunday schools, worship services, religious education, and family and cultural life construct God in various ways for the contexts in which we live. As we mature to adulthood, our life experiences enable us to deconstruct and reconstruct those images which have come to be integral to our lives. As adults, we choose either to make these our own or to reject them.

The history of Christianity illustrates how images of God are constructed over a long period of time. From the historical Jesus through the faith experience of his first followers, we receive a faith-informed impression of who God was for Jesus and his first followers. Writing down their experience of Jesus, the gospel writers provided believers of later periods with various God-images that reflect the experience of the communities for which they wrote. These became the framework for later experiences of people who lived in radically different times and cultures. Each period provided different viewpoints, insights, and practical images of this God manifested in and through Jesus who, for Christian faith, became the Christ. Various periods of history accented one perspective more than others. Sometimes it was God the compassionate Lover, or the merciful Forgiver, or the fearful Judge. Throughout this historical process, whatever the image, it came to be identified with the religious institutions which preached God as they saw God to be.

Various historical and cultural events precipitate the development of organized religions into structured societies. As with all institutions, structural organization often goes hand-in-hand with corruption, which means that as organizations, religious bodies are constantly in need of reform. It would seem today that many religious organizations are in a self-preservation mode. In the case of Christianity, this means that churches can often lose sight of their original inspiration, Jesus himself, who came to reveal a path to full human living. As a result, Jesus is sometimes presented more as a dogma than a person who lives with humanity in a continuing dynamic of love — being with, suffering with, rejoicing with, and loving with all human beings.

Throughout the two thousand years of Christian history, various people have emerged to call the churches back to the heart of belief in this living Lord, Jesus the Christ. One of these was a sixteenth-century Spanish mystic, John of the Cross (1542–91). In his *Ascent of Mount Carmel*, he addresses those seeking visions and miracles. John notes that not these, but Jesus and the God he revealed are the core of Christian faith. John writes about this as if God is speaking:

> If I have already told you all things in my Word, my Son, and if I have no other word, what answer or revelation can I now make that would surpass this? Fasten your eyes on him alone because in him I have spoken and revealed all and in him you will discover even more than you ask for and desire. You are making an appeal for locutions and revelations that are incomplete, but if you turn your eyes to him you will find them complete. For he is my entire locution and response, vision and revelation which I have already spoken, answered, manifested, and revealed to you by giving him to you as a brother, companion, master, ransom, and reward.... Hear him because I have no more faith to reveal or truths to manifest.... Behold him well, for in him you will uncover all of these already made and given and many more.[61]

John of the Cross reminds us that who God is is found in Jesus, whose fundamental teaching was Love. In fact, for John after we die God will evaluate our lives on the basis of love alone — our love for each other, the world about us, and the God we meet in relationships and the world itself.[62] This is indeed the core of Christian belief, the very reality of the God made known in Jesus.

Today, however, we need only turn our television sets to various evangelists to find a God who is sometimes not recognizable within this authentic Christian tradition of a living God who is Love. Here we often hear of a judging, battering God who seems to want only to catch us in wrongdoing and to punish us. This is not a God of love, but of punishment. Despite some individual churches and clergy who present the loving God of Christianity, gay men and especially those living with HIV/AIDS have heard little else than hatred spewed at them in the name of Christianity. It is a wonder that they have any belief in God at all. Yet, many partners and those to whom they give care maintain faith in a God, or a transcendent, loving Power who remains with them.[63] This God touches and remains with them despite those who profess to be God's messengers and proclaimers of the Good News of Jesus Christ.

Let us now listen to the stories of these partners as they speak about how they envisage (or do not envisage) God, and how they relate to God.

Stories of God

God: Compassionate and Loving

Like many gay men who are out, Jason encountered people who felt that God condemned him because he was gay. Each time, he thought, "who is this God that people are talking about? It's certainly not the compassionate God that I know." In living his life, especially after his diagnosis with HIV/AIDS, he came to understand and relate to God differently than he had before. Jason was often asked to speak to students about being HIV positive. During his presentations, it was not unusual for people to question him about his relationship to God. When one young woman asked, "Do you think there's a place for you in heaven?" he answered, "Well, you know, I'm open to the possibility there might be." When she revealed the prejudice behind her question, Jason responded, "You know what? I don't know what your views on God are, and I don't care. But God has been very good to me. He has blessed me. In fact, I think I do his work. I try in every interaction I have with another human being to make it better. This whole thing about heaven and hell, I have a feeling it's the same place. I think we're all going to end up together because we're all together, here and it's going to be heaven for those of us who didn't think we were going to make it. And it will be hell for all of you who acted so badly and rudely in this lifetime."

Though there was an edge to his response Jason's impatience still manages to sketch clearly the God he had come to see over time. He had found a God who loved him and Karl. He realized that this God so loved them that God dared to suffer with as well as be happy with them. This moved Jason to relate to others in a way which would provide them with wholeness — to act toward others in a life-enhancing way. Jason's relationship with God changed his life, and he shared this change with others.

Todd, whose accident had left him in a wheelchair, related to God as "Someone who is there to watch over and will accept you when you leave. I hope my friend is with this God, and when my time comes we will rejoin, pick up, and go on together." For Todd, life with his partner might seem to have been absolutely destroyed by death. However, because he saw God as one who loves and cares about all human beings, he felt that he and his lover would one day be together again. They would pick up where death had forced them apart, because God loved them and the whole of humankind.

Approaching the mystery of death, people dealing with terminal illness find a profound challenge to the meaning of their lives. Coping with the horror and sadness of a beloved's death sometimes ushers in a renewed relationship with the Transcendent whom those grieving experience as immanent. Reflecting on Louis's death, Cyril found that "God is love. God is all the energy that keeps this earth going round and round. God is all that's good. God is here on earth...but I don't think that God is a man or a woman. I don't know what he is. To me it's an energy and we're all part of that energy. You're part of God. I'm part of God...all of our energy put together becomes a greater force." God's presence everywhere provided Cyril with a sense of community rather than the isolation death so often creates. He found sacredness in people and creation — a sacredness which resulted from the reality of God's intimacy with all. Cyril also sensed that Louis was with him, for if God was indeed loving energy, Louis could not simply cease to exist. He said, "When Louis died, one day or a few days after, I went outside and I said, 'Louis, give me a sign.' I was in the backyard and I saw a falling star. Then I went to the park a few days later, and I was talking to him. And then I saw another falling star. Things like this...you feel there is something else." He saw. He felt. In an event which might simply be a natural occurrence for some people, Cyril found a sign of his connection of love to Louis and to God.

The sense of the presence of a similar God filled Rick as well. "On a personal level — God is a loving father, a supporter, a comfort, an infinitely lovely being. On a larger level God is the creator. I believe that in everything that occurs he is present and that we as human beings are important to him. I believe that we were created to have fellowship with God, and I don't think there is any higher calling in the universe." In God the constant lover, Rick found an incredible intimacy and mutuality. God was not someone out to get him, but one who offered a deep, loving relationship of presence. From that presence, Rick found strength to continue living life fully.

Yet, he saw that God was more than just someone for him alone. God lived in and loved the whole world. In everyone and everything, God calls all persons into that loving relationship. The dynamic of the Godlife takes hold within human experience, not apart from it. Fellowship with God is not merely institutionalized religious activity. Rather it is life lived in such a way that we discover the beauty of all its elements. Even the tragic can contribute to the beauty of life if we dare to look. While such a perspective does not remove pain and anguish, it has the potential to unleash the wonder of presence, as it did for Rick.

Such images of God do not take shape overnight. They are the constructions of lives lived by each of us. Lou had been part of the Salvation Army, and he noted how his description of God had changed since his childhood. "I believe I've grown. I think they're stagnant. I might sound judgmental, but so be it. I like where I am." He spoke of God in terms similar to Rick's, but added "God to me is probably closer to goddess. I find the feminine, encompassing, loving nurturing type of God is the person I worship. What we consider as feminine qualities, I see in God. These are the things that attract me." Some find a marvelously appealing tenderness within God, a God who caresses and establishes a relationship of authentic mutuality. God is the lover who provides life not just by giving birth, but by continuous nurturing to empower a person to become fully human. In fact, this God frees us to live and be God in the world so that others may come to know God as lover, nurturer, life-giver.

Because of so many false prophets in organized Christianity, too often this God as "goddess" fails to come through. Lou said, "The Christian type of God that deems that a certain code is necessary to your behavior or belief, I can't accept. God is a nurturing, loving entity." For Lou, the rather common image of God as a legalistic, punitive being who preserves order and the comfortable status quo is merely the projection of various religious leaders who need to dominate others. Gay men have been too oppressed by various religions and power structures to find much within them which is helpful to human living. Gay men cannot find such a God of control helpful in their quest for the sacred mystery of life. Instead, the God of Love draws them to a wholeness in which they integrate both their masculine and feminine components. Gay partners of lovers who live with HIV/AIDS commonly seek an authenticity that deconstructs the stereotypical God of fundamentalist hatred, power, and control.

In the church where he grew up, Duane saw a stained-glass window with a portrait of Jesus with his arms outstretched. That image remained with him into his adult years. It continued to be the basic image containing qualities of the God in whom he believed. "God is a guide, a counselor, a conscience, compassionate and helpful...all the good qualities that you look for in people. God's in all of us — that's how I feel — he keeps us on the right track, understands and is there." Faith in this God empowered Duane to be "kind and compassionate and all those things we can forget about in a busy world." Faith was for Duane not just intellectual acceptance of a creed or dogma, but living contact with a God who kept him in touch with how to be really human in his interrelationship with others. His image of God had grown as he matured, yet it had clear similarities with the God he had come to know as a child.

If Duane retained to a large extent the image of God he had found in his childhood religion, Claude found that with age and experience his notion of God changed. "God is someone that's present always in my days, in my dreams, and I still believe that God created me. I feel closer to a certain God. I used to believe a lot — in a different God. And since I have been diagnosed, that's changed. I feel more comfortable with this God. I try to see God changing me every day. I feel I'm a much nicer person than I was and that I'm wiser than I was. I try to be." Where before Claude might have done things for others out of fear of punishment, now he would do simple things, he noted, like smiling more at people out of entirely new motives. "It's not because I'm afraid and I'm doing it consciously — doing little things to have God more on my side. It's with no self-interest that I do these things. I just feel that that's the thing to do and I do it." The comfort Claude found in a loving God who remained with him enabled him to reach out and provide others with support and encouragement. His belief not only sustained him personally, but allowed him to relate to others in a more loving way so that they too might find happiness in situations which hardly seemed to allow for joy at all. Faith that moves a person to create a fuller life for others is one that is consonant with the life of Jesus as recounted in the Christian gospels. Living for others is an authentic embodiment of Christian spirituality.

One day when I visited Claude in the hospital just a few days before he died, he sat in a chair and I was next to him. We sat together watching a snow storm so thick it obscured the beautiful view of the tall buildings in the distance. Claude's lover, Shaun, stood nearby. Claude could not speak, but was fully conscious. Our right hands were joined. Occasionally I would say something to him, and he would try to form words. But we both knew that speech was not necessary. When I told him that I had to leave, Claude would not let go of my hand. He gripped it harder. Then, after a few moments, he tapped my hand and released it, and I kissed him goodbye. The next time I saw him, he was in a coma. We never spoke to each other again. I remembered our day sitting together and how without speech he had communicated to me and to Shaun how much he loved us and wanted to make us happy with his weak smile and touch. He both held on, and let us go, knowing he would see the God who had been there with him and who had taught him to love others in simple ways.

All these gay partners, living with HIV/AIDS in themselves and/or their beloved found a God who was personal, loving, and deeply compassionate. Through dark and questioning times — times of solitary suffering of real doubt and anguish — they emerged knowing a God so loving that it gave them new insights into life and relationships with others. As their love for their partners deepened, they found God more deeply. This God was profoundly involved in their love for each other. God's love moved them into deeper relationships with other people as well.

God as Relationship

Over time Ken came to see that his God could be found in people. God was "you and me. There's a little of God in every one of us. God is present in each of us. God is with and within each of us. We are created in God's image, not by God as a separate anthropomorphic being, but by God in the sense that we humans create one another, not only physiologically but also socially and culturally. God creates gay and lesbian people just as solidly as anyone else is created. We are goodness and right in God's sight. There's no reason to be ashamed — we are what we are. God's presence is most strongly felt when we're together, both in relationship and in social relationships. There are times when people gather under the wrong circumstances and for a while there is more evil than good present, but all in all there is a spirit working among people. We use the language of God and try to use it as a gender-inclusive term. I recognize the language of Buddha and Mohammed as just as valid. Wherever one finds one's symbols, leaders, or examples of that spirit, I think that's valid and good and should be celebrated." Our interrelationships enter into the whole process of becoming who we are. Within the whole dynamic of interaction that forms us and others as persons, God creates and is present. Gay and lesbian persons are an integral part of the divine collective creation, and not only is God present in them, but God loves them as God's own image.

For Ken, we sense God's presence precisely in the love we experience with our lovers and others by whom our lives are shaped. This Spirit of God found in relationship cannot be extinguished. God's commitment to all people and things remains constant, deep, and passionate. That consistent presence is at the heart of the wholesome relationships which gay partners establish. Their sexual giving and receiving finds at its heart the God who is Love. Their concern and care for each other enfleshes God's care and concern. All this becomes their response of love to the God who created and is within each human being. Such a notion of God opened Ken to see that we experience the touch, the presence of the Divine in models of authentic spiritual life. Everything and everyone in creation are sacraments of a God whose presence is constant and whose love creates love in and for all. In pointing to such a God, the sacred words of various religious traditions offer a wholeness to all who seek it.

Greg highlighted the depth of God's presence in relationship when he said, "Where did I feel the greatest experience of God? The greatest experience of God I had was in our lovemaking or in cuddling each other. We'd wake up in the morning and cuddle each other for twenty minutes to a half-hour before getting out of bed. In that cuddling I felt a deep sense of prayer, presence, and encouragement. I really felt Christ's presence being embodied in our touch. It was a kind of prayer of presence and silence. Perhaps my own Ignatian sense of finding God in all things and finding God in this illness was there. When I say God is to be found in the faces of HIV people... it was very real for me in terms of Al. I found Christ in him and in his struggles as an HIV-challenged individual. He was someone I loved, and here was Christ." Gay partners like Greg remind us of the beauty of bodily relations in love. In our society sexuality still tends to be something "not quite right." Too often people see it as something which should be hidden and fail to realize that it is an essential and profound reality in every person's life — indeed the deepest expression of our love for the other. It is the place where we are totally vulnerable and where we give and receive the intimacy so essential

to our human development. It is not only about reproducing physical life, but about giving and receiving life in its deepest meaning.
Our sexuality empowers us to create the world, to provide meaning
and hope for all people.

In his sexual lovemaking, Greg found that Christ is present in the
love spoken by partner to partner. In Christ God affirms the wonder and dignity of the human, the embodied, the enfleshed. In so
doing, God conveys that all experience, events, and people are sacred. The great mystics such as Ignatius of Loyola, John of the Cross,
Hildegard of Bingen, Teresa of Avila, Elizabeth of the Trinity, and
others constantly remind us of the mystery of the sacred in all that is
human and, indeed, in the whole of creation. To enter into the fullness of love — which sexual lovemaking is at its best — is to find at
its very core the God who made it so. The integration of body and
soul constitutes an authentic spirituality which many gay partners
find as they journey with their lovers living with HIV/AIDS.

Human relationships are, then, the quintessential place of encoun-
tering the Divine. Darin explained his way of knowing God when
he said, "I think we find God by helping others. I find that when I
really give of myself I receive twice as much in return. In this time
when I've been in pain and trying to find my way, if I see people
lost on the way, I try to help them. I recognize pain in them and
try to offer them some guidance. I find that I'll figure something else
out. Through that I'm finding more and more — maybe instead of
myself — the God, a God, or our God. And using my talents, such
as piano playing, doing things that are completely charitable, pretty
amazing things can happen. I think it's the essence of sharing what
we've learned or what we have with others selflessly. And if we trust
in these things, if we have faith, we'll be fine. But I'm still working
on that." In moving out of ourselves for the sake of the other, especially the other who is suffering, we discover something or someone
beyond and yet within. In that movement in caring, the person finds
a God who is alive and not just some dogmatic formulation about
God. The movement of caring creates life for the other and for the
self. Every human being longs for relationship, and when gay partners find this in their lover or in doing something for one isolated in
pain, the barriers of self are broken and God is found, along with
meaning and life.

Jack spoke of God as being found everywhere when he said:
"Who is God? I don't know if I believe in the classical bearded
figure sitting on a cloud. I see God in lots of things. God is more

like people, relationships, places, things. People do incredibly awful things to each other, and I've seen people do incredibly wonderful things for each other. God is probably also somewhere in me too." For Jack God is a presence we see when we open our eyes to what surrounds us. To look honestly at life and relationships empowers us to see there a God who can do nothing else but love. God's constant presence is never obliterated by the "awful things" human beings do to each other. God remains dynamically alive in the "incredibly wonderful things" we do for one another. The universal presence of God in the whole of creation means that each person has the opportunity to find God and who God is.

God Is Everything

North America has been enriched by the Native peoples who inhabited the land long before any white settlers arrived. Their spiritual traditions have provided all people an opportunity to see the earth in a new way. While the white missionaries attempted to change their perspectives and religious beliefs, the Native people kept their traditions alive for the most part. Though raised a Catholic, Steve tapped into his own Native roots to find a God more meaningful than the God he had previously been told about. He said, "I call him the Great Spirit, the Creator. But for me it's still the same God that everyone believes in. The earth, nature itself is God." Grounded in the sacredness of creation, Steve's culture enabled him to see God's presence in the trees, in animals, in the earth itself as well as in people. This challenged him to live in harmony with all life, for it all was God in a very real way. This God transcended whatever name people might give to God. Thus, connection with this God provided him with a sense of oneness with others, regardless of their cultural or religious background.

While Keith's background was Christian, he became disillusioned with the notions of God presented to him. In the Native traditions he found something which rooted him in the sacredness of the universe. Keith spoke of the life surrounding us in nature and how it is important to respect and foster it. "That's really hard to put into words," he said. "I don't think there's one single power or entity that controls everything. I tend to think we have to do our...Pass. I can't go any further." Though Keith could not express the relationship of the earth and God which he sensed within himself, he affirmed that, somehow, everything was connected.

For some, God is so present, surrounding the person, that God is imaged as energy and power. Stan saw God this way. "God is the source — the energy. God is the source of all things. Maybe it's all the miraculous things that surround us. It's the life force. I look at God and the power of God as all the good things." For him, everything flowed from God and remained in God — the trees, animals, people, nature as a whole. Goodness is at the heart of all things that are and that goodness finds its source in God. Thus, to become conscious of the presence of all that forms our day-to-day life is to become conscious of God. Even more, when we enter into a relationship with people or things we are entering into a relationship with God. There is no separation between people and things and God. Being the source of their very existence, God constantly touches human beings who become conscious of things around themselves.

In any spiritual tradition we find great teachers constantly reminding us to live consciously in the present, for in so doing, we live more and more consciously in God who is in the reality of the now. Seeing God in this way was Stan's spirituality — his integrating process in which God became constantly more present at each moment of his deepening awareness. Yet, because he realized that evil also exists in the world, Stan's notion of God as source and presence of all goodness also moved him to action for good. "I think we're here to make the world a better place if we can. That's how I feel about everybody." Being in relationship to God as the good is not simply an intellectual activity, but creates in one the urge to passionately create transformative goodness so that life becomes more human for all. Such is the calling of the human being.

Chris saw God in a similar way. "God is mind, spirit, soul, life, truth and love. God is everything that is — the only creator, source, and power. God is all that is, and that's what I try to focus on all the time. My only career is to express God." With his realization of the intimate bond between creation and God, Chris sought to establish his life in relationship to the God of love and truth embodied in creation. This was not a relationship focused on sin — fearful and ridden with guilt. Rather it was one of deepening gratitude to a God who so loved humanity and creation that this God created and lived in it all. As with other partners, this realization challenged Chris to be God for others. Expressing God was not the preachy witnessing so often confused with religiosity, but was Chris's attempt to embody God and become a sacrament — a visible sign of God's ever-present love and goodness. From this flowed a spirituality of creating goodness and love for others, as God does.

Grant's illness and death were the context in which Paul shaped his image of God. "I still find it very difficult to believe that there's a God that's sitting there controlling or has control of all of this. But I do find it very possible to believe in a force or some controlling factor. At the point in time when Grant died, if God worked into it at all — it was because he was someone I could be angry at." While Paul believed that there was something somewhere which made things ultimately turn out for the best, for him God was not someone out to find problems with a person's sexuality. Rather for Paul God was someone who accepted him (and others) "for what I am and who I am, and for my mistakes, my errors, the things I do that don't fit into someone else's ideas." It is this unconditional love that empowers a person to develop fully. Paul realized that his life had not always been the ideal, that there had been mistakes. Perhaps he had used people. Maybe he had not been kind and considerate. But whatever his mistakes, they could not destroy his relationship with God. For Paul God was someone who accepted him as he was. With such a notion of God he could find empowerment to change what needed to be changed and enhance what was positive within his life. Even when other human beings could not accept him as he was, his God was one who fully accepted and, indeed, loved him.

God as Unknown

Some partners suspended all affirmation of God in any form. Because of several negative experiences with organized Christian religion, Shaun wanted to have nothing to do with Christianity. While his partner, Claude, had come to a deep, loving relationship with God, Shaun said "I have really no perception of it [the divinity]. I guess I'm what you'd call agnostic. I don't deny it. I just don't know, and I have no idea." While some "believers" might write Shaun off as someone without a value system, this was not the case. Shaun expressed his deep humanity in his love for Claude as well as in his relationship with friends and family. He lived his life authentically and with real love. As a gardener and interior decorator, he relished the enjoyment others found in his creations. Shaun and Claude entertained their friends in an atmosphere of acceptance and love, and in doing so revealed the best that belief in God offers the human community. This is not to trivialize Shaun's agnostic stance. Rather, it is to affirm that suspension of belief does not preclude a person's embodying real human love, or living an authentic human existence.

Dave maintained that he was an atheist. However, when asked who God was for him, he answered "We're all God or God is in all of us. God is also a composite or all of us. Whether it's God or something, I feel there's something looking after me, and yet I also feel that God is out there and is not interested in our daily lives. We're not that important." Dave's suspension of belief did not thwart his affirmation of the divine core of every human being and thus the sacredness of all things and people.

Frank was much like Shaun. As he spoke of who God was for him, he responded: "I don't think I can answer that. I don't want to say I don't believe in God because I'm not sure if I do or not. Actually, I'm going to church now. I never used to go to church. This time I decided instead of going to a Catholic church (I am a Roman Catholic), I decided to go to an Anglican church to see the difference. So, I'm still evaluating. Too many things were said when I was a kid. A part of me is at the point where I want to make a decision on this on my own because I'm too screwed up around 'this is wrong' and 'this is right.' I want to know the reasons for these expensive churches." Even if he exhibited a real hesitancy in affirming a God, Frank continued his searching. As for others, the early experience of a judgmental God offered by organized religion became a block in a conscious relationship with God. Frank's searching, however, revealed a commitment to authenticity. If ultimately he found God, he would embrace that God. If not, he would continue to live his life with the core values which he maintained. As is commonly said, it is by their fruits that you will know them. Whether people believe in Jesus Christ or in God, if we see positive and constructive contributions to life and the world within their lifestyle, they are indeed on the path of a deepening spirituality which enhances not only their own lives, but the lives of the community as a whole.

Prayer-Connections

Throughout the story of humanity, there has been a consistent belief in some kind of transcendent power or personality. Following upon the affirmation of a deity, human beings have always attempted to communicate with that deity. Various Native traditions throughout the world have consistently developed rituals composed of words and symbols drawn from their culture to enter into communication with the sacred. Human beings are essentially relational and hence require a means of communication with whatever or whoever they enter into relationship with.

In fact, every human being is constantly in the process of communicating with others. We are a constant word to the other whether we are conscious of it or not. Our body language speaks who we are and who we see ourselves to be. When we consciously engage in the communication process, we direct our body language and words in ways which most appropriately speak our innermost selves. Through our words — whether speech or actions — we authentically express the persons we are. In fact, words at their deepest level are meant to speak the self. When there is a response in like manner from the other we have real communication — union with the other in the one reality we share. When the other is the Transcendent, that process of communication is called prayer.

From the Native traditions of North America to tribal traditions in Africa and Asia, the whole of human history is filled with the sacred grounding of communication with the Transcendent. Sometimes complex, sometimes simple, the process has involved both communal and individual elements. In the case of a communitarian action, rituals have been developed in which someone chosen by the community seeks to accomplish connection with the sacred. In these, shamans, priests, imams, or rabbis became the go-betweens of the Transcendent and humanity. In the pre-Christian Philippines, particularly in the northern tribes, these mediators were of two special types, women and homosexuals. For their communities, they exhibited unique, life-giving sacred capacities. In other cultures a variety of human beings have received special recognition as intermediaries.

Most cultures have also recognized that the individual can communicate with the Divine. From their communitarian and family forms of communication individuals have developed rituals and other means to touch the Sacred Transcendent One(s). These forms have flowed from who these individual persons were and have expressed their identity as they contacted the divine realities. Such communication is deeply personal, then, for it is the expression of unique individuals enfleshed in words and rituals.

In Christianity, as in other religious milieus, people have practiced prayer as a special means of entering into a union with the Transcendent. The great mystics of the Christian tradition have taught a process of prayer focusing on relationship to the God manifested in Jesus the Christ. Augustine, Bernard of Clairvaux, Teresa of Avila,

John of the Cross, Ignatius of Loyola, Thérèse of Lisieux, Elizabeth of the Trinity, Dag Hammarskjöld and countless others have left accounts of how one can enter into that special communication process called prayer. For these Christian mystics, all human beings by the very fact of their being are meant to be in relation to the Divine, and prayer is a special way in which we can actualize that relationship.

The gay male partners whose stories appear here are no different. In their faith (and even sometimes within their suspension of belief), they relate to God (however they see God), through what we call prayer. They do this using a variety of notions of prayer.

Prayer as Conversation

More often than not, people think of prayer as a form of talking with God. Jason found that his relationship with God expressed itself in informal conversation. "Basically, it was just a conversation that I would have. I would just say, 'This is what is happening, and I don't understand it?' I was a little bit of a smart ass, but I learned you can be that with God because he's going to know anyway. So I've learned to just talk to God, and even now I make a decision. And I leave it. I put it up to God." Jason spoke of a time when he wanted desperately to move back to the island where he had grown up. By the time he had left to visit there, he said, "The answer which was very clear was, 'Not yet.' And so, I didn't move." Finding that answer meant that he had to listen. "When God speaks to you, listen. And God speaks to me quite often." Such listening is not an attempt to hear a disincarnate voice which gives answers or statements in a vision or through other extraordinary means. Rather, for Jason, listening meant being open to situations in which he found himself, and gradually he would "hear" either a confirmation of his decision or the need to change his mind.

People might say that this has nothing to do with God, but everything to do with being reasonable and considering the various elements of a decision. But Jason saw his decision making colored by his faith in a God deeply interested in his life who remained intimately involved with him in the daily events of his life. Prayer was a relationship in which God and he were partners in the ongoing reality of life. It required his action of speaking and listening. Through listening to the events in his life which he could interpret as ways God was counselling him toward the best path, he made his choices and lived them. Faith is what makes this relationship and interpretation of events possible. It is faith, too, that makes people aware, like the prophets of old, that we can be ourselves with God. We need not cower in fear before an Almighty. With Jason, we understand that God loves us so deeply that we can be angry with God at times, as well as relax with God. Prayer is expressing who we are with our God, as we are at any given moment.

Rico spoke of how he would pray when Jon was ill. Drawing upon his earlier religious tradition, he spoke of how he would often pray the Our Father. "But mostly prayer was talking to him. During all of Jon's illness I would ask him to keep me strong and to keep going and keep Jon from suffering. It was selfish. I asked him to keep us together as long as possible. I would pray at night asking for answers. And the answers I would get I wasn't aware of. At one point he went into a coma and they thought he was going to die. He had the last rites....Two weeks later he was sitting in a chair visiting with his brothers and sisters. I remember the first meal he could eat after that and I was so happy. I was thinking maybe he'd have another six months." There is a certain sense of comfort in resorting to what provided us with security and peace in the past. Often traditional prayers like the Our Father do that. This traditional prayer affirms that God cares, that God's compassionate love will not leave us.

Rico's love for Jon was so strong that he did not want their relationship to be crushed by death. He saw this as "selfish" because it was something he wanted for himself, even when perhaps death would have been better for Jon, with all the suffering he was enduring. Jon's partial recovery came as an answer to Rico's prayers, even if he was not immediately aware of this. For Rico God was real and in relationship to him just as his situation with Jon was real. His faith in this loving God enabled him to live out that anguished situation of his lover's illness as fully as possible. His prayer was the bond that joined him and Jon with God in a conscious way.

With his evangelical Christian background, Rick spoke of prayer as very informal. "A lot of times it's like talking. There's no formal ritual like the Our Father or ten Hail Marys or the rosary. I usually start with 'Heavenly Father.' Sometimes it's just thanking him for what he's done for me. It's not anything grand or miraculous. But I always close my prayer with 'In Jesus' name.' I believe that Jesus is with us in all our ups and downs." Where formal prayers are helpful to some, an ordinary conversation works well for others. In such ordinary talking with God, one finds a deep faith in a God who really cares about and wants to be with us in whatever happens in our lives. The realization that God remains constant in our times of joy and of utter discouragement opens the door to saying to God whatever one feels. For Rick, Jesus was so intimately connected with him that all that affected him affected Jesus. Such living connection to God in prayer enables us to cope with the suffering that occurs in day-to-day life.

Sometimes, and perhaps very commonly, partners pray constantly. As Luke said, "I pray constantly.... I'll speak to God. The God I love and worship does not force himself upon me. He's always there. I know he is. He will always take care of me. I communicate with God. It's like a conversation." There is a freedom in such a relationship with God. God remains with human beings in a way similar to a lover remaining steady whatever he is undergoing in his relationship with his partner. As in such a relationship, one's thoughts turn to God, and this is praying constantly. One can talk with God about everything — and about nothing. Just as lovers sometimes talk together about important matters and at other times about rather meaningless things, so do we speak with God. When God is important to us, we feel free to be with God in prayer which expresses who we are in this relationship at any given moment.

Praying also means being aware of God's presence. In Greg's relationship with God, there were various opportunities for prayer. "Prayer for me has several different components. It has the component of lovemaking. Actually in the passion of lovemaking, I would frequently have the image of Christ being there. I also tend to pray in the shower. It's a good way to start the day. It might mean becoming mindful of God's presence throughout the day. I also meditate, read the scriptures and celebrate the Eucharist. I offer the Ignatian prayer 'Take and receive.'" There is nothing in our lives that is not sacred and cannot be an occasion for prayer. Because of the negativity our culture attaches to sexuality, we often think that making love cannot express a positive relationship with God. However, in many partners' experience, it is in making love with one's partner that the deepest prayer and deepest union with God takes place.

Our union with our lover is our union with God. Throughout the whole dynamic of our physical expressions of love, we express our love for each other — marvelous, delightful, and pleasurable as it is — and in these expressions we make love with God. This becomes our prayer. Moreover, something as banal as showering can offer us time and solitude to become conscious of God. Walking along a beach or a forest path or hiking up a mountain: these also are times loaded with potential for communing with God. Through the practice of communing with God at such times and in such places, we develop a sense of God's continuous presence in us and in all human beings.

Foundational to such encounters with God are more formal occasions such as meditation, scripture reading, and eucharistic celebrations. These focus our minds on how God has related to us through our believing ancestors and in the story of humanity. We discover in such practices a God who has always been there with humanity, a God who has touched persons in a variety of ways. We come to realize that this happens to us as well. Then, when thoughts of God enter our mind during the day, we know that God is coming to say "hello." Such touches make us more sensitive and alive to the sacredness of all our human experience. By being aware of this at certain privileged moments, we see the sacred dimensions of all those times which we simply go through without really paying attention at all.

Prayer as Petition and Thanksgiving

Communicating with God often includes asking for something or being grateful for special people who have become an important part of our process of becoming of who we are or for events that have occurred in our lives. With such forms of prayer, however, we need to reach beyond the "Candy Machine God," God as the magical wizard who will fulfill all our whims. The relationship implied by such images of God is utilitarian, an "I-It" relationship. Were we to relate to other persons in this way, it would not be long before the relationship would end.

Jess, who had been raised in a cultural tradition which accented fear of God, found that his prayer during Max's illness centered on asking God to give Max faith so that he would not be condemned. "I think fear was a much bigger emotion. I'd say that in a way my faith, my religion, which is very different now than then, kept me going." At the time, he prayed out of fear of that "almighty, powerful God." This was Jess's way of coping.

Later, after Max died, Jess came to see the inauthenticity of such a relationship with God, for God was one who loved him and Max. He labored under the oppressiveness of religious teaching which insisted that God was determined to punish anyone who did not live according to laws which his church told him were God's laws. This imprisoned him in fear of God rather than opening a relationship of love. The whole life, suffering, and death of Jesus speak of a God of love, not of power, punishment, hatred, and condemnation. Yet Jess and others whose religious upbringing was determinative labored greatly under the stress of trying to satisfy the ceaseless, impossible demands of the un-Christian gods presented by many individuals in various churches which claim the name of Christian. For Jess, time and experience refashioned his notion of God as he came to communicate with a God of love as others did.

For Duncan, whose ordained ministry remained central in his life, prayer had a contemplative dimension. He found that he became more and more conscious of God's presence deep within himself and within the world which surrounds him. "I pray contemplatively, using traditional and some other forms. I pray formal prayers in liturgy. I do healing prayers, which have a specific focus in laying on of hands. I often reflect, do a reflective type of prayer right in the middle of everything because it's one of the ways I get myself centered." Contemplation means being open to and receiving from God whatever it is that God offers at any moment. In the process we become deeply aware that we are not alone. We sense not only God's presence in contemplative prayer, but sometimes the presence of other people and things which may not be physically present at that particular moment. Contemplation connects with all that is.

Duncan felt strongly that such contemplative prayer could provide healing for himself and others — not curing, but healing. He had founded a healing prayer group, which focused on the laying on of hands. Here, touching the other and being touched became the outward sign that no one was alone, but all were intimately connected with God and all of humanity. Duncan saw being physically touched by others as a sacrament of being touched by God. Such sacramental touch enables us to see how important everyone is in the cycle of life and death. In this healing circle, participants could relax and allow the power of all to enter them, providing peace and hope that all was well despite whatever one was suffering.[64]

Keith found prayer centered on "thankfulness each day that I'm alive to witness whatever happens and protection for Sloan and me. And for both of us to live a good quality of life." Such prayer cherishes the insight that every moment of life is precious. Prayer rises from the depths of our existential situation. When life is appreciated, we know that nothing is superfluous or unimportant. Everything takes on a sacredness. With such an attitude, we discover the beauty and wonder of life everywhere, in the delight found in a pet dog, as well as in the majesty of magnificent sunsets or the power of crashing waves.

More particularly for partners who live in the context of HIV/AIDS, gratitude for each day of life together is profoundly important. Consequently, prayer becomes a dialogue expressing this thankfulness to the God seen as having made it possible. For Keith the spirit of thankfulness predominated — thankfulness that he was alive to experience whatever the new day would offer Sloan and him. Whatever life brought, they would be alive, with the potential to deepen their love as they lived it together. From this hope flowed the petition that they be protected to live yet more fully with "a good quality of life."

Like Keith, Frank centered his prayer on helping his partner, Fabian, through the terribly painful times he was experiencing. He prayed "a lot. I just prayed to God for Fabian not to suffer too much, especially when he was in pain and especially when certain things happened. . . . If you want to know how I asked, I said, 'If you're there, if I can take a burden of the pain that he has, if I can take it upon me so that you can remove it from him, then let me take some of the pain away.' " To see one's lover suffer as AIDS takes over is incredibly painful. One's helplessness in the face of suffering becomes the stuff out of which prayer flows. Uncertain that God is even present, the caregiving partner seeks to alleviate the pain, to free the partner from part of what he is going through by carrying some of it within oneself. Frank and Fabian had shared all in their partnership, and now Frank was coming to realize that the journey Fabian was on was one in which their sharing was ceasing. This part of the journey, Fabian alone could travel. Here was the core of Frank's pain: he could be there with Fabian only from the outside. Frank's prayer expressed both his pain at this separation and his desire to be part of Fabian's pain.

Connecting with God can occur through a variety of means. Harry said that he had prayed that Bobby would die because this is what Bobby wanted in his pain. Harry recounted how he prayed. "I sat on a beach for three days and did nothing but meditate. I got a great deal out of listening to *Into the Woods*, which is one of the most spiritual shows I've ever seen. I saw it in New York before. Bobby did too and brought the CD home. Bobby didn't get it at first, but then I discovered every time I came back home that he had played the CD during the day. It deals with the collective unconscious. It was enormously useful to me. It was a source of meditation and prayer just to listen to the wonderful human ideas and wonderful music. Music is another way that I pray. It's a way of meditation for me — to listen to music, and not necessarily religious music. I mean all kinds of music." For some people, nature can be what calls them to consciousness of God. For others it can be visual art. For still others like Harry it is music in all its forms. The CD with the lyrics of *Into the Woods* became an instrument of a meditating process which was his prayer, his connection with the Divine; it was as well a means of effecting a special connection with Bobby, who had attended the show with him. Prayer unites people not only with God but with each other in an ever-deepening spiral of love.

Prayer also creates a space in which presence is enhanced. Ken noted that he and Lewis prayed together in an informal way at meals and other times of the day. But there were times when they would have "a more formal prayer time when visitors were there, visitors and colleagues who were comfortable with it. He died the Wednesday before Maundy Thursday. We had friends around his bed for what we called a time of prayer and presence. Lewis was unable to communicate, but you could see in his eyes that he knew everyone was there. Everyone took turns speaking a few words of remembrance or sharing something they wanted to say to him or about him. We sang the Alleluia that he had sung in the congregation, and then we prayed the prayer of Jesus together. And it was a time of great presence." Since both had been seminary students, they were naturally comfortable with prayer. Prayer was something that brought them together and enabled them to gather others into their love. Thus, they gave visitors the opportunity to be part of that presence together through some "formal times of prayer."

The most striking of these gatherings took place when Lewis was close to death and Ken and their friends gathered around him to affirm their relationship with him and his with them. This is precisely what prayer should be — a connection with the Divine among others. Even so-called "private" prayer is never really solitary. In it, the one who prays joins with the whole community of humanity. When we pray, we enter into communion with a God who is with and in all persons and indeed the whole of creation. The group who prayed with Ken and Lewis consolidated their relationship and support with prayer. In this bond Ken sensed a "presence" linking them at a very sacred time of life, the time of a person's death.

Prayer in Native Traditions

As we have noted, finding themselves immersed in an alien culture, many Native Americans are rediscovering the depths of their Native beliefs. Having resisted religious and governmental attempts to make them into "white people," they have delved into their own history and culture to find dignity as Natives. Those who have retained the sacred mysteries and language of their people become bridges to a healthy life and spirituality for other Native peoples. Such bridges are important since the process of christianization of Native peoples often lacked a sense of inculturation to enable the real gospel of Jesus Christ to be lived within various cultures without destroying them. The missionaries often falsely understood the gospel as purely white and very European. They then proceeded, albeit with good intentions, to make the "savages" civilized — meaning white, European Christians. In the process, they ripped apart the dignity of the Native peoples and replaced it with guilt for one's indigenous culture and beliefs.

For gay Native men like Steve, who had left his people while very young and tried to make his way in the non-Native world, there is a twofold oppression — that of being a Native and a gay man as well. Steve's Catholic upbringing made things worse. When he had reached a point where he felt totally lost, he met Sean and started on a road of self-affirmation. Gradually, he found his Native religious beliefs provided him with a new positive view of God and of himself. While Sean was ill, Steve prayed, but "it was the Native prayer that my sister gave me. The last lines are: 'Make me ready to come to you with clean hands and straight eyes so that my spirit will come to you without shame.'" This prayer became for him a new way of seeing and being with the Great Spirit, the Creator. "These were really strong words that I could understand. It was the biggest help I got. I felt my sister came on the scene in time to show me this. She gave me a book and wrote something in it. I'm beginning to learn more about Native religion." His prayer related him to a God who loved the whole of creation and opened up a world inhabited by the spirits of that same God. Moreover, this God actually loved *him* as a gay Native man with a lover. The prayer became the impetus for Steve to learn more about the sacred traditions of his ancestors, hoping that these would open him to an even deeper spiritual life. The words of the God the missionaries had presented to him did little for him, so intermixed were they with negative attempts to tell him that he was no good simply because he was Native and gay. Now, he began to see the world in a new way, to see that he, with all that he was, formed an essential and good part of the world.

Dennis had been raised a Roman Catholic, but his church's stance on homosexuality made him think that he could not be a real part of the church. He was not only gay, but was also a Native person, and like Steve he came to see both as good. To be authentically who he was, he had to claim his identity. In the Native tradition Dennis found a loving Creator God. He speaks of how he prayed: "I used Catholic prayers I was raised with, but I also used my own words to talk to him. I expressed how I felt, what I needed." Prayers from his childhood became a way to say who he was in relationship to the Creator who filled the whole world with that sacred presence to which he felt deeply connected as a Native American. Consequently, he felt free to speak with this Great Spirit in his own way as well. Prayer was for Dennis a way of consciously relating to God. While he was close to his family, he had lived most of his life outside his Native milieu. Yet, he had begun to discover the treasures of that milieu and to see how they empowered him to live fully as a man both gay and Native.

Prayer as Living Life

In religious traditions lived authentically, prayer has never been limited simply to reciting words. The world's religions recognize that words can be more than words. They can effect within a person and a community what they signify. They can express who we are at any given time and can create within us a transformative way of seeing and being in the world. Prayerful contact with God enables us to claim this vision of the self and the world. One who prays sees the goodness of each person and all humanity, for authentic prayer indicates a vision of the intimate interconnectedness of all. It furthermore engages us on a path of continuing pursuit of wholeness for ourselves and others, for as we become who we were meant to be, so does the other grow in proportion. Prayer is seeing and engaging in life, rather than mere words recited by the person of prayer.

Cyril expressed this when he said how he prayed while Louis was ill: "I prayed a lot and still do. To me praying is not only getting down and praying. Every nice thing you can do for other people, that's prayer. Even when I cry because I'm sad and I miss him, those tears are prayers. They're love. The way I pray is I try to be good. I'm not always good." There is nothing that is not capable of being prayer. Every element in life contains the potential for communicating with the sacred. That potential is actualized when we see and affirm the goodness surrounding everyone in life. Trying to be good means trying to incarnate the positive elements in our own life and the life of the world. We may not always succeed, but the effort itself becomes a connection to the life that is God.

With his Asian heritage, Soko discovered a sense of praying in the moment that enhanced such connectedness: "I pray life, just close my eyes, try to feel the connection. I don't need to chant, though chant is prayer too. It helps me. So if I feel I need it, I will use it. And also, I don't go to any specific church or religious group. I don't pray as they do or I don't follow the rules that it should be like this — you bow three times, you clap your hands twice. I don't do that anymore, but when I go to nature, go hiking, to the beach, it's my way of praying. I may sit down and feel it." Whatever enables us to sense the connection with something or someone greater than we is capable of being prayer. Rituals in various religious traditions have always been there to enhance that possibility of connection. Yet when they threaten to become fossilized they need either to be dropped or reclaimed in their original sense. Soko found nature one of his best "sacraments" of prayer. As he connected with it sensibly, he found his relationship to the wider web of life. Everything that exists carries within it the potential of connecting the human being with everything else and particularly with God, the Creator, the Great Spirit, the Lover, the Father, the Power greater than self.

While we all have has different images of God which each of us express in a unique way, it is clear that one's own story influences these images and expressions. In these stories of gay male partners, what is remarkable is how, for each one, God is one who offers humans an intimate relationship. The God of these stories is not some ethereal, distant being overseeing the order of the universe. Nor is their God one who cannot feel and change. Nor is their God a hateful judge who makes them tow the line of regulations made by ordinary mortals. Rather, their God lives with them in and through all the events that make up who they are. Their relationships with their lovers are the very stuff of their process of human development. These same relationships in the context of HIV/AIDS create the possibility of seeing God in ways that often transcend what they had been taught by institutional religions.

For many, God becomes the lover filled with compassion, a God who feels with them and suffers with them, who rejoices and makes love with them as they make love with their partners. The partners have come to realize that nothing is outside the sphere of God's relating with them. God is one on whom they can rely even if things do not get better as their lovers approach death.

Some spoke of God as power and energy, as a transcendent reality. Even so, they perceive this God as consistently related to them in their lives. Life itself bespeaks this Energy. Thus, everything has its own mystery and sacredness which these partners respected. With them, nothing of this divine energy can be discovered outside a conscious awareness of every given moment and every given being with whom they come into contact. Relationship consciously lived creates their lives. Through their choices they seek to enter life as fully as possible and there discover meaning. At times, meaning seems overwhelmed by tragedy. Yet in many of these stories even tragedy ultimately contains sparks of hope which empower us to go on living the adventure we call life.

Those who suspend judgment about the existence of God or Power live their lives with their lovers as fully as others. Even after their lovers had died, they continued to experience the sacred in time. In living, they search, perhaps unconsciously, for what life has to offer in terms of some kind of meaning. For these partners, life is more than the absurdity which some have experienced. They continue to live, and their lives are their search for what they instinctively feel is there even when this presence hides itself.

Depending upon their images of God,[65] the partners whose stories we have heard also communicate with God. They pray. Sometimes they use formal prayers recovered from their childhood. Sometimes they simply talk with God, expressing their fears, hopes, dreams, and desires. As in all relationships, they sense the need to open themselves to the other. Everything can be a call to prayer as they listen to what surrounds them. Listening to the events, people, and things in their lives, they find a call to speak with God. In living their lives consciously they know they are praying. Their expressions of gratitude or anger empower them to live.[66]

The partners to whom we have been listening pray as they love the world around them. They pray as they make love to each other. They pray as they listen to music. They pray as they reflect upon life. Formally or informally, they relate in various ways to God, and this is their prayer. In living their lives as gay partners, they offer life to others through what they experience.

Chapter 7

Sharing Hope: Some Advice

If living in a time of HIV/AIDS has taught us anything, it has taught us that we're in this together. It is a community affair. To be human means to live within community, where we find hope, strength, and meaning. But is community possible? One wonders when one sees the violence and injustice practiced by human beings against each other. Structural evil afflicts every society. Is it possible to fashion an authentic human community where everyone counts and all are made to feel that their contribution can make a difference? Perhaps we who believe that such authentic human living together is possible are just dreamers. Or are we?

The stories we have heard throughout this book tell us that community is possible. The gay male partners have created community by daring to live together, by living their lives honestly, and by sharing their stories. They form part of a long history of small pockets of humanity that have had the courage to live for one another and that in so doing change society little by little into more authentic community. Great figures such as Buddha, Jesus, Gandhi, Steve Biko, Martin Luther King, Dag Hammarskjöld, and Oscar Romero have been part of this history. Each of these challenged society to live in a fully human way by recognizing that we are all interconnected: when one suffers oppression, we all suffer. Others who through their lives and writings have left us a similar legacy of courage to change what needs to be changed include Madeleine Delbrêl, Marguerite Porete, Albert Schweitzer, Thomas Merton, Teresa of Avila, Simone Weil, Edith Stein, and Dorothy Day. Within the gay community such visionary shapers of a more authentic human existence have included Michael Callen, Randy Shilts, Harvey Milk, and thousands of unrecognized lesbians and gay men.

Many so-called unknown people also contribute in profound ways to making us more human. Every one who has lived has left a mark on our lives. Time may have rendered many silent, but their silence still speaks in our lives today. My ancestors who left France in the early seventeenth century to make their way in New France amid hardship and danger are my roots in life. My grandparents who moved to the United States at the turn of the century to work in the cotton mills and shoe shops of New England bore the brunt of discrimination and virtual slave conditions. They are my roots. My parents who struggled with poverty provided me with a truly human atmosphere of love and concern for others. They are my roots. All of these in some way or other humanized the world, my world and yours.

I would like to think that the AIDS epidemic, which the entire human community is experiencing, has brought out the best in many of us. In the gay community, lesbians and gay men have come together to show that community in the best sense is possible. In doing so, they have in turn become a challenge to churches and society to build authentic community. As the stories we are hearing reveal, the lives of gay men and lesbians are often significant monuments of such community. These stories demonstrate that authentic community comes into being when people are permitted to find meaning in their lives by being true to themselves and sharing this meaning with others.

This is precisely what Jesus of Nazareth did. What he learned in his formative years — how to love and be human — he offered to all humanity. He was a dreamer who thought things could be different, that human beings could really live in concern for each other. On the basis of what he learned in his life, he offered advice. Basically, this "way" that Jesus offered centered on two pivotal realities: authenticity and love. Being who one is means daring to claim and affirm oneself. In doing this one entices humanity away from inauthenticity and hypocrisy. This is the first essential step in building community. From there, people must realize that all persons are of utmost value, that we are to love unreservedly. If we dare such love, we may, of course, be crucified. But as the way to wholeness for the human community love will ultimately win out. Such was the belief of Jesus of Nazareth: the world will be changed by each person's determination to be authentic and loving.

The gay partners we have heard broke silence so that others would know from their experience what it is like to live in love. Their experiences offer humanity some steps toward realizing community. When asked what they would recommend to others in their situation, they had fascinating things to say. Listening to them we are challenged to open our lives, to live the dream which provides hope and constitutes community.

Recommendations

Choose and Follow Through

We often go through life without sitting down and really thinking about what is happening. So many things preoccupy us — our
jobs, relationships, finances, and future plans. In fact, most of the
time we tend to live in the future or the past while the only real
thing — the present — goes by without a glance. Yet the reality is
now. It is important to live the now with all that it contains. For
this now contains the potential to ground us and enhance every moment of our lives. This does not mean that we should not think of
the past or make plans for the future. However, through this living in the present we realize that the past is over, and that what
we plan for the future does not yet exist. Sometimes a crisis is what
forces us to look at who we have been and are now. Then the meaning of our lives might become a pertinent question for which we
realize that we need to find some answers. For the partners, diagnosis often brings such a crisis of meaning. It forces them to look
at life and make choices they might otherwise have shuffled into
the shadows.

Jason spoke of taking on the responsibilities which such a choice
entails. "You can spend time thinking of all the injustices and how
unfair everything is as you try to live your life. I've learned, no matter what you think, it doesn't change a whole lot. No matter what
you think of your circumstances, they don't really change unless you
do something about it. I think I learned it. Your frame of mind really
has a huge impact on how you live your life. And if you don't want
to do something, if you don't want to be a caregiver, you don't have
to be. But know that if you make that choice you are taking on a
huge responsibility. And you can just handle whatever is placed in
front of you. I think of those things. You know that God never puts
anything in front of you that you can't handle, that you're not ready
for. . . . When I speak to groups, I say, 'You're all artists in this room.
Go out and create your masterpiece. Just do something. . . . Don't let
your life pass you by so that you can look back and say "God, I
should have done this." ' "

Sometimes the idea of having to care for one's partner who is ill
can seem overwhelming. Most gay men have seen friends or acquaintances become ill, suffer extremely difficult times, and die. They have
known what caregiving involves and how difficult it is emotionally
and physically. Yet it can be done and has been done. If one chooses

to go ahead, Jason thinks it will work out. What is needed is an attitude that one will do it.

But such intensive caregiving certainly cannot be done alone. As Jason said, "Get real. Get help. I've always been blessed because every time I have a crisis in faith or something, the right person shows up with exactly the right thing to say." Often, the help we need comes at the right time. This does not mean that we just sit and wait. Sometimes we have to go out and ask for help. One may be afraid, but with determination everything will work out in the end. Jason reminds us that each person is an artist. By living our lives responsibly we make them dynamic pieces of art for ourselves and others to find hope in whatever our lives contain.

Even after we have made the decision to be there for our partners, the task can still seem overwhelming. But as Rico noted, "We're really a lot stronger than we think.... All I can say is that if you really, really, really want to do it, just do it. I promised myself I was going to care for him no matter what. What got me through it was seeing the beauty in it. I don't think there's anything wrong with somebody who can't do it. That's fine. But if you're going to do it, do it with your heart and love and do it with a smile.... Really, really, really listen. Listen to yourself and your partner. There's a lot of beauty out there. You can see beauty in anything. I saw beauty in coming into his world. Look for those little things that you might miss. Even in the hospital I would try to feed him sometimes, and sometimes he didn't want to be fed. He'd close his eyes and pretend he was sleeping. Then from the bathroom, I'd see in the mirror that he was watching — his eyes were open. I would think 'Oh, you're so cute.' "

Once again, determination accompanying a choice is essential. It is quite possible, however, that though someone loves his partner deeply, he is unable to assume the heavy responsibility of caregiving. It is important to know that it is all right to make such a choice. The choice to provide care or not requires that one be very attentive to oneself and one's partner. To force oneself to assume the burden of providing care will mean constant difficulty and pain for both the caregiver and the one who is ill. For those who can assume this burden from the heart, it is life-giving. As Rico notes, one finds beauty there despite the suffering of the person one loves. Listening and seeing the "little things" creates energy to go on whatever happens. None of this takes away the pain one naturally feels watching one's lover suffer so much. But it does make it bearable — for oneself and for the other.

Attentiveness to his own feelings is absolutely essential to the partner who takes care of his lover. Sloan emphasized this point very strongly: "It's okay to feel whatever you feel. If you want to go out on the back porch and let loose with a big Carol Burnett–type scream, that's fine. If you want to cry, that's fine. Feel what you feel and let that happen. Don't bottle that stuff up because it always gets so perverted in the system when you bottle the emotions up. But once you've let those emotions happen, don't start planning the funeral. Don't hear the HIV diagnosis as a death sentence — contrary to everything our culture says, what our media say. Be stubborn enough about it. I'm convinced of the mind-body connection. If we start giving it mental and emotional consent it will more likely have its way. I want to hear the grief and anger, but I also want to encourage them to have enough faith in themselves and their relationship that they can do it together. Don't make it be a death sentence for each other and the relationship."

Our social formation often keeps us from expressing our feelings. Far too often we are taught to suppress and hide them. But it is essential that we recognize our feelings if we are to be healthy human beings and thus form healthy relationships. To some, Sloan's advice about not allowing diagnosis to be a death sentence might appear to be denial. It is in fact a way of coping and creating a better quality of life for his relationship, even in the face of HIV. The new drug combinations hold much promise, though they may not work for everyone. But if lovers can maintain a positive outlook, it will help. Even when a cure does not occur, healing can and will allow the life of love to deepen. Should no cure result, one should not feel guilty or say, "Oh, it's my fault. I didn't maintain a positive attitude." It is important that the lover be there as he is at any given time. And that means being there with his feelings, his hopes, his despair, and above all his love — however it is that both can express their love for each other.

The experience of caregiving for a partner with HIV/AIDS involves depths of feelings that we might never suspect could exist. The caregiver wants nothing less than his lover's return to good health or positive quality of life. When the lover seems to give up, this can be profoundly discouraging. Or if one's lover expresses anger at one's attempt to keep him alive, a variety of feelings can come to the fore, some hardly even guessed at before.

Frank said: "I think I would recommend that these people be quite aware of the amount of patience and tolerance that is required. If they don't have that, they need to be sure to work on it. You have to be able to love your partner to get through it. A lot of understanding is very important." At times, the lover may not speak. There are times when he may want to eat something special, but after his partner has gone to the store and prepares the food, he may not eat it. Frustrated by his weakness or pain, he may vent anger at his partner-caregiver. In turn, fatigue, fear, powerlessness, and a host of other forces can make the caregiver angry. At all these times, a superhuman patience is needed. What is required is the attempt to understand the lover's life from inside. Understanding that frustration comes from the disease and not from the suffering person helps. If the caregiver has someone with whom he can share his frustration and fears, this will help immensely. It may be a nurse who comes in, a member of a support group, or a friend. Whoever it is, we need to realize that we are all in this together and our relationships provide the strength, patience, and determination we need to continue loving through it all.

Seek Help

At the beginning of the epidemic no one really knew what would be involved in caring for a lover who had become ill with AIDS. In fact in those early days, once full-blown AIDS developed, life expectancy was limited to a few months. At that time AIDS was a death sentence. Lovers became frightened and overwhelmed. Some left their partners. Others stayed and did the best they could with few available resources. With the exception of rural areas, by the second decade of the epidemic all kinds of organizations, support groups, and nursing assistance became available for those living with HIV/AIDS. Furthermore, despite a few lean years, research developed and continued to make advances so that today, with the new drug combinations, many persons living with HIV/AIDS have much more quality time. They even have hope that this might become a treatable chronic disease. Although many unanswered questions remain, we now know a great deal about the disease and how it develops. This knowledge alone has alleviated the fear of the unknown for most partners. If they live in or near urban areas, they also have access to help, and it is help that is most needed, at some periods more than others.

Most of the partners who spoke of advice they would offer to others living in similar situations underlined the need to seek assistance. This was the first thing that Duncan said. "One, don't try to do it by yourself. That's the major thing. Two, make decisions together that are for the good of both of you. Three, get your paperwork in order." It can be overwhelming to hold down a job, take care of one's lover, keep house, cook, bring the lover to doctors' appointments, and find people to sit when one simply cannot be there. Trying to do all this alone will destroy a person and have devastating effects on the relationship, leaving both the partner and his lover with intense frustration and possibly guilt. Caring for oneself is essential if both are to have quality time together. Otherwise, it is not long before proper care cannot be provided and the health of both deteriorates. There are times when the caregiver needs a break. He needs someone to talk to as well. Realizing his own needs, he must seek out someone who is willing and able to provide the respite needed. No one can go through this alone.

Second, Duncan advised that the partners discuss together things that need to be looked at. Living a shared life, the caregiver and his lover need to talk about what both are feeling and what both would want done in various circumstances. Then, when the lover cannot make decisions, the partner can do so without feeling that he has to decide crucial things all by himself, with the hesitations, fears, and guilt that might be associated with such decisions. If they have talked things over together and understood each other's wishes, it becomes manageable, if not easy.

Third, Duncan brought out the need to get the "paperwork in order." Wills, financial and medical powers of attorney, legal documents relating to possessions common to both (such as the house or furnishings) need to be attended to before the partner becomes ill.[67] This can prevent major problems when severe illness or death enters the picture. Duncan had encountered some problems because he and Cliff had not discussed all the issues together beforehand. After Cliff died, Duncan had to deal with some financial problems which otherwise could have been eliminated. Duncan was extremely sensitive about this particular issue of legal resolutions to problems and wanted others to make sure that they had things clearly set in order.

Darin noted that a person should "not try to do it completely alone. You need a break every once in a while, like calling a friend." He too spoke of the need to talk together. "I think the thing I'm very happy about is that when Emile was still alive we talked about our mortality. A lot of the things we talked about gave me a pretty good sense of what he wanted to do. It gave me a lot of strength. Don't be afraid of talking about these things. You talk about them on good days. We talked about death. We cried together too. Without that, people don't have a sense of the other person. Then when the person is gone, life falls apart." Such open dialogue is very important. But it is not easy. Sometimes the partner does not want to bring things up for fear of upsetting his lover, or the lover may hesitate lest he worry his partner. Then, nothing gets said, and the very intent to protect each other causes more pain and grief for both. When the lover is very ill, it is not a good time to raise the questions that need to be raised. So, as Darin noted, it is best to talk about the difficult things when the lover is well or relatively so, "on good days." What is left unsaid can become very problematic, especially for the partner.

While getting help from others is clearly essential, Todd maintained that what matters most is to "keep a close bond. Do what you can. Get outside help like some care, music, etc., but stay involved. Don't close the door. As sick as he is when he looks into your eyes, even though he may not say anything, your souls, I'm sure are together." Partners who have lived together have spent time consciously or unconsciously bonding together. They have shared hopes and dreams, fears and sorrows, angers and frustrations, their bodies and souls. It is important to keep the process of bonding alive even when the person is very ill. That bond provides a means of communicating with the other even when words fail or are no longer possible. To see that his partner is near, to feel his hand and caresses, provides the lover with a sense of much-needed peace. Even surrounded by friends and chosen family, their relationship centers on what is between them. It is upon this bond that their life as one is founded, and it needs to remain strong.

Even when difficulties arise it is important for the couple to protect the bond that holds them together. In some cases, for example, the lover's parents may intervene to stop the partner from visiting or being there to care for his lover. This creates unthinkable pain. Even less drastic actions, such as words and gestures which suggest the parents' dislike for the partner, can harm their son, for he and his lover are really one. The bond they have established in their living together is paramount.

Because of his experience, Stan felt deeply about "the importance of people helping, people coming by just to visit, people you can talk to even if they're not close friends, people who maybe have been through this before, people who can be a sounding board. You need someone you can talk to. You get so tired sometimes and exhausted. You know you're giving your best, and yet you know what the end result will be. So you're heading for this disaster ahead, but all your energies are going into taking care of the other person. It's very dangerous territory. I think people who've been through it, could probably help. I would have appreciated that, some people who had experienced it before and who could give me a lift. Many times I would be alone with Mario for weeks on end. I didn't have a lot of people coming around. Sometimes, especially during radiation treatments, he would sleep around the clock, and I would be wandering around trying to find something to keep myself entertained. It was hard sometimes. It would have been great to have someone around to talk to."

For Stan, people who had been in similar situations could help simply by being there to listen and to provide support. It was only after Mario died that Stan started going to meetings for caregivers and partners. Interacting with others who had gone through something similar helped Stan to see how important such support would have been for him during the actual process. He also knew that anyone at all — close friends or not — could provide relief. All he needed was someone with whom he could share what was going on within himself at the time of his caregiving. Stan's advice is in fact an invitation to people who know someone going through a partner's illness or loss to call or visit. On such visits, one need not worry, wondering, "What will I say or do?" As Stan emphasized, one need only let go and be there for the other.

Chris spoke of the need to find support, but he added: "I would certainly recommend that they pursue a spiritual avenue whatever that might be — to develop a spiritual connection. I would recommend a support group because there's a spirituality there as well. I also made a decision to volunteer with a relationship-support group." Whether or not that spiritual avenue is theistic or religious, it is helpful to find it and enter that process. Finding meaning, integrating it, and creating community with other people deepens our perspective and increases the possibility of developing our humanity.

As we have seen, authentic spirituality connects one to the human community in concern and compassion. For those in gay relationships, the relationship is the basis for spirituality. An authentic spirituality increases the love the two have for each other and maximizes the meaning of their physical lovemaking. When it takes root, their love for each other moves them to share their compassion and concern with other persons.

Greg too emphasized spirituality as a need. "I think the need for support groups for lovers of HIV spouses is essential. And it needs to be set up in a way that contains a dimension of spirituality. Spirituality as a resource is underutilized. Probably that's because of the ambivalence in our community toward institutionalized religion.... Not everyone has training in spiritual direction. Some of these resources need to be made available." Greg touches upon the suspicion of spirituality found in certain circles in the gay community because of their identification of spirituality with organized religion. Yet no religion has exclusive rights to spirituality, which is first and foremost a human reality. Spirituality at its best empowers the human being to live fully here and now this enfleshed life. Providing means for lovers of HIV partners to tap into this element so essential to truly human life is a role that some support groups are beginning to take seriously. But those who do this are still few and far between.

The spiritual connection could really be what enhances a lover's relationship to his partner and vice versa. Authentic spirituality does exist within the relationship of two gay men consciously seeking meaning which they then try to enflesh in their lives, and this spirituality needs to be nurtured. It is life-giving. Such a spirituality will affirm their sexual union. It will not demand that physical lovemaking stop. It will be a spirituality that enables the couple to see their relationship as positive and valuable. Such spirituality will move them out of isolation and into an affirmation of all that is beautiful and good in the world — a world which is within the orbit of their care and love too.

As Dave proposed that laws should be changed to provide full support to gay male couples, he also noted the need for the caregiver and his lover to have support, very practical support: "When somebody's sick all the time, the partner becomes nurse. The roles change and you don't get to spend time as a couple anymore. So it was really nice to have somebody there to do laundry and cleaning so we could go and do something as a couple and try to maintain a relationship as a couple — not as invalid and caregiver." Partners need help so that they can spend time together. Friends, relatives, and other support-givers should be cognizant of this. Their very practical help can mean that the two men can have valuable time alone together, perhaps to go for a walk along the beach, or to window shop, or to have dinner together. Friends can be there not just to provide relief for the caregiver, but also to help so that the lovers can have some special times together as well. Partners may ask friends for this kind of help, but when friends can foresee the need, it is even better.

Opening Communication

Darin emphasizes how important it is for partners to really talk about things. Couples who have tried to do this over the whole of their relationship may find it easier to speak about difficult matters than those who have placed less emphasis on such sharing. Most long-term relationships have lasted and developed precisely because the lines of communication remained open. In such relationships, one often develops a sense of what the other feels without the other saying anything in words. Having come to know each other, lovers develop an innate sense of what the other experiences and how he reacts. There remain, however, things which both find very difficult to share. When HIV/AIDS enters the relationship, it becomes even more important to discuss what may have simply been put off before this. Now, issues surrounding the partners' life together — illness, treatments, death — take precedence. Depending on the level of communication they have developed, it may be extremely difficult if not impossible to bring these to the fore.

Keith spoke of relationships and how essential it is for the lovers to share their feelings. "Relationships — seropositive, heterosexual, whatever — they take work. You have to be willing to love yourself and your partner enough to work things out. Sloan and I were starting out late on that. You've got to have the bumps in the road in order to work things out, but you can't be afraid to talk. You have that communication line open. And you do not necessarily agree all the time. There are times when you don't. In fact...I thought anonymous sex was fine, and he was coming from the monogamous side. That resulted in some good banter. We had a good time with that....It's not Sloan's theology or Keith's theology. They really are molding into one through communication work. And I think that's where a lot of gay couples don't stay gay couples. We feel you have to be friends before you become lovers. We didn't see this at the time. The gay population has it backward. You go and have sex first, and then you try to become lovers. It doesn't work. At least, it didn't work for us, and from the bad relationships I've seen in the gay and lesbian world it doesn't work that way."

The communication process requires primarily a foundation and atmosphere of love for it to succeed. When difficulties arise ("bumps in the road"), love provides the possibility to face them openly. Then the disagreements which develop are challenges to growth. When the "lines of communication" remain open, both lovers can come to know not only the other, but themselves as well. They come to face what they did not want to address previously, or it may be something which either one or both partners had no idea troubled them. Their interaction in the relationship can provide the light to see and resolve such matters. This does not mean that they will ultimately agree. But it does mean that they will see things more clearly and thus enter their relationship with a clearer vision and a more profound sense of all that they bring to the relationship.

In this way the relationship can become more authentic, as both come to see how they "are molding into one through communication work." For Keith and Sloan, their life together and their communication brought them to understand something that they had not appreciated before. They had started their life together with sex, and friendship came later. Through their sharing they arrived at a point where they believed that friendship should come first, and then sex became an expression of that friendship, which was primary. They could not have come to that conclusion unless they had been willing to express their divergent views on that subject. While there are gay men who will radically disagree with their conclusion about the primacy of friendship-love, the point is that lovers have to share their views in order for their life together to take root and deepen. To find meaning in life, couples need to be open, little by little, with each other. Then together they develop a spirituality as one and not as two individuals.

Relationship is built through daring to be who we are with the other. This involves risk to the extent that we do not know how the other will react. Dennis recommended "that you be very willing to be open with each other, that you share and express all the things you're feeling, that you not be afraid to express something because you might hurt the feelings of the other or because you fear being rejected. Also you should not be afraid to cry with each other. I really found that helped a lot. It showed Hal how deep my feelings were." There are real risks in saying everything to one's lover, yet it is taking the risk that enables relationships to take root even more deeply.

Expressing oneself as fully as possible is essential, as Rick noted. "Talking, finding out what you can about the realities of what

you're dealing with, not the emotions or the paranoia only. Find
out what it is you're dealing with. Learn to express what you feel.
It's okay to be sad. It's okay to feel helpless. It's okay to feel lonely
and angry. Express it. Talk to your partner and to your friends.
If that's not available then talk to somebody from the AIDS committee or a buddy. Psychologists can help. I talk to them as well,
although that can be constraining. But don't be afraid to express
what you feel. Men are generally taught from childhood that you
don't show emotion. That is crap. You have to express what you
feel and you have to talk to your partner. You have to. You have
to have that. If you can't do that, you have to learn. You really
have to learn. You can't go through something like this with him
in that corner and you in another corner. So talking really helps."
It is only when we really become involved with another person that
we find out who we are. When two lovers live and love together,
the other's reactions create a question not only about who he is,
but about who I am. In communicating with the other, my identity
becomes clearer.

Lovers are sometimes, then, like rough stones placed in a polishing
machine: through friction the rough edges become smooth and the
individual beauty of each is brought to the surface. In relationships,
this is not accomplished overnight. It is a life-long process of daring
to look at and claim who each one is. It is essential to dare to feel
everything and bring it to the surface by sharing it with the other —
sadness, loneliness, anger, fear, hope. There may be circumstances
that prevent one from sharing such feelings with one's lover, but they
can be shared with someone else. In such openings to another, one
sustains relationship and prepares the gift of self to be shared with
one's lover later when the time is ripe. In a healthy relationship the
battle corners must become places of meeting and growing rather
than isolating fortresses where we hide ourselves.

Lou developed the theme of communication while accenting the
need to avoid regret about things undone or unsaid. "One of the
things I would recommend is so simple that it's almost obvious.
That's to say and do the things you think about when the chance
is there. You will not get an opportunity to say or do things after
your partner is gone. I think one of the most significant things we
did was to take a spur-of-the-moment trip. It was two weeks before
he went into the hospital. I remember thinking after that, 'If I hadn't
done that, he wouldn't have enjoyed that day.' For the most part,
I always communicated to him my feelings for him. Tell him you

love him. Tell him how much he means to you! You won't get that opportunity afterward."

The chance opening for communication may come when your lover says a few halting words about how he wonders if the disease is progressing. Or there may be a time when your partner tries to say how much you mean to him. Whatever the occasion, it is important to let the sharing unfold and to reciprocate.

Lou applies the same principle to "doing." "Do the things you think about when the chance is there." There may be all kinds of reasons for not going on a trip or for a walk or shopping. But one often discovers that now is the right time to act; the rest can wait. Doing even little things together can be as important to building a loving relationship as verbal openness can be.

Doing can also mean letting the lover do what is good for him. Jack noted, "One of the first things we did when Jerry was diagnosed was we both went to a counselor. I found her to be tiresome. I went once. Jerry went several times and said he felt she helped him. That might be advice for others. I let him do what he felt he needed to do. I went with an open mind and heart, but I didn't feel any kind of release, but Jerry felt better and seeing that felt good." Prior to this, Jack had said how important it was for a couple with one partner HIV positive to "sit down and talk to each other about their hopes and dreams." For his part Jack first talked to God and prayed that the whole thing was a mistake. Later he came to accept the diagnosis and offer as much support to Jerry as possible. When his reaction to the counselor was negative, rather than discourage Jerry, he let go of his own feelings and allowed Jerry to continue to do what was good for him. Communication allows both partners freedom to pursue paths that are good for them.

Communication does not mean only talking. Nor is it talking *at* the other. It is a dialogue which requires receiving as well as giving. Ronald underlined this: "It is above all to listen. So that the person feels worthwhile. You look for something that the person holds as important. That must be respected. For example, if he wants to wear nice clothes, if that can make him feel worthwhile, encourage him. Let him do it." Ronald noted how Kerry wanted to hide his illness and wearing nice clothes gave him that sense of protection. "There is no sense in putting a stick in the spokes. Even if we know it doesn't make sense." Kerry did drag, and Ronald was afraid that doing the shows would wear him down. It made no sense to Ronald that Kerry continue performing. Nevertheless, Ronald was always there at the performance. Despite his misgivings, Ronald realized how important it was for Kerry to perform, whatever the consequences. He had listened to Kerry's unspoken words and respected his decision. It is only in listening to the desires and hopes of the other that one can enter the other's life. Communication involves deciphering what is not said or cannot be said. Partners can communicate not only in words, but in deeds as well.

Live Life

When two people in a relationship find themselves in the context of HIV/AIDS, they understandably find their lives overwhelmed with fear and a variety of emotions. With the diagnosis, there is the fear of impending death and separation. However, it is important to move beyond that and find quality times together.

Keith spoke of really living life: "Being HIV positive is not a death sentence. I believe that wholeheartedly. I don't want to say don't think about it, because some people say that's running away from it. But why dwell on it when there are other things out there that you can better put your energies to?" With the discovery of effective new drugs, this advice seems more to the point than it was several years ago. A positive frame of mind helps both partners to live fully now. When one concentrates upon AIDS as death, too much psychic and physical energy is drained off and opportunities for a rich life together are missed.

Concentrating on AIDS as death can lead one into making decisions which otherwise one would not have made. Today, with the advance in treatments, many people with AIDS find their lives back on track and are faced with decisions they never thought they would have to make again. Cyril offered very important advice: "To those people who have just found out they have AIDS — don't stop living, don't quit your job, don't sell things you have that are dear to you." He spoke from his own experience, since diagnosis had led him to start shutting down and making decisions about not getting on with life. "But it is not the end of the world to have AIDS. Life is a privilege. It's also a privilege to be sick because you learn things and you discover things inside you that you never knew were there. And they just come out and I surprise myself." Some might not agree with Cyril about sickness as a privilege. What he means, however, is that if we live out our lives at any given time, we can always find something which provides us with insight.

What Cyril says about persons diagnosed with HIV/AIDS is true for their partners as well. Whether one's partner is very ill or relatively healthy, he is still alive. When we cherish life, we seek to find beauty in it and to accent that. Partners can do things that underline the fact that love continues, that the sunrise is still awe-inspiring, that people are there interacting and loving. Discovering or rediscovering the good things of life promotes healing. Each couple needs to discover its own balance and path. But when a couple turns outward and contributes to the beauty of the world in whatever way their personalities and physical conditions allow, they will find deeper life. The meaning they will discover in the process will enhance their life as a couple and as lovers.

Steve emphasized the need to search for one's own meaning rather than letting others impose meaning on partners living with HIV/AIDS. "Don't believe it's happening to you because of your life. We've had plagues all through history. I've heard people say this is a punishment from God — stuff like that. It really affected me at the beginning. I really thought this was my fate because of the way I lived my life. But I think there's a reason for everything, and if you look hard enough you'll find it. Life is like that. There's hard and there's good. It's not good all the time. So accept things and search for the reasons. If you find the reason, it will give you a lot." Disease is not a punishment from God. Those who affirm this have failed to know a God who is pure love. The goodness and difficulties of life are part of a life cycle that unfolds naturally.

Steve urged people to look for meaning — and particularly the depth of meaning — in whatever happens. Despite what others say, we each must find the real meaning of our own life. In the process of seeking that meaning, it is important that we love ourselves as we are. That entails being gentle with ourselves as we search for that ultimate meaning that opens up new doors to living. As this happens, we find that God, or the Transcendent Power, or Energy has been there as a love which never falters. Meaning, life, God — whatever name we attach to this — become the filter which empowers each of us to live authentically and fully here and now.

Duane reflected on a similar theme: "We all get a hand dealt to us, and I believe we get the tools to deal with it. . . . I've had shitty stuff happen in my life. Everybody does. I don't think my life's been any better or worse than the average person's. You wonder why some people seem to get an awful lot, but I always found I had the ability to deal with it or at least the resources to know where to look

for help if I couldn't deal with it. But I think God gave me those
kinds of abilities and the rational thinking to do the right thing. I
think I've been given these tools and that keeps me sane...able to
handle life in a productive way." While he found what he needed
to deal with negative aspects of life, he also noted a mystery which
perhaps can never be resolved: why do some people seem to have it
so bad in life? While there is no answer to this, we can certainly say
it is not God who imposes the difficulties we face. When we meet
people in horrible situations, we are dumbfounded, speechless, and
powerless. At such times, we are thrown back on mystery with the
question, "How is this possible? Why?" All we can do is be there in
support and hope that life is not totally meaningless. Such situations
call forth our compassion, our ability to suffer with the other. Then
we are joined in the humanity which we share in a mystery beyond
our understanding.

AIDS: A Special Meaning?

We all relate to AIDS in our own way. Because we are all different, our approach to it and the experience of it have very individual
characteristics. When asked whether AIDS had a special meaning for
them, the partners responded in a variety of ways, and some stated
that it had no meaning or no special meaning for them.

Love

For Jason, AIDS became a challenge to dare to be free to love. "I
think basically it just boiled down to love. 'Either I love you or I
don't. I can give you my love knowing that you're not going to be
here forever.' I think it meant that it gave us permission to do whatever the hell we wanted. And no one questioned it. And so it was
a permission to live." Living in the context of AIDS, he and Karl
found they were free to choose whatever they believed was form-
ing their life at that moment. For them, love took prominence. Now
their love had new parameters, and the choice was theirs to continue or to end the relationship. Once Jason made his choice to love
whatever the end result, this unleashed other possibilities which now
could be chosen within the context of the initial love he had affirmed.
As a result, he could say that the meaning of AIDS was love.

Darin expressed a similar notion of the special meaning AIDS held
for him. "I think but for the disease that would eventually take him,
we wouldn't have taken the time in loving each other to the fullest. I

think that's why we had respect for the feelings of each other and the sense of each other: because we didn't have a lot of time. We didn't have until we were sixty to develop those feelings for each other. We tried just to celebrate what we found in each other. Actually, I think if Emile was around now and there was no disease and we were both fine, I don't think it would have gone this quickly. I think that adversity brings out the best of what I am." As with Jason, AIDS became the catalyst for Darin to take a serious look at where he and his lover were, particularly in their relationship. Because of its presence, AIDS compressed their life together into a shorter period, and they tried to make the most of it.

Learning the Value of All

After Jon's death Rico initially felt that his life seemed to have no meaning. He wanted to commit suicide. But then as he thought about how important Jon had been in his life and how he had affected him so much, he found something which opened doors to new meaning. "I try never to take anyone for granted now. Sometimes I took him for granted when he was alive. I'll never take anyone for granted again. The major thing is all the walls and all the shit I went through all my life — this wall that I created to protect myself. He broke it. I can cry and it feels great — freeing and liberating. And there's a certain sadness and irony that it took his death to wake me up. I think he was really happy with me, and he loved me the way I was. But I think now I would be his ideal. I'm seeing someone now. It's not a big, big love. It's not what I had with Jon. I can lie in this person's arms and enjoy it. I couldn't do that with Jon, you know. So his life and his death — if I can't learn from that, how many more chances am I going to get? He was the calm. Boy, did I cry, and I still cry. I thought it was too late, but it's not too late."

It is not unusual for someone to see values in a relationship only after one's lover has died. For Rico, the discovery was that the relationship had provided him with a freedom he had not experienced before. Jon had torn down the defensive walls he had built up around himself to keep from being hurt.

Having taken this for granted during Jon's lifetime, he came to realize that he should try to see things as they were — limited and temporary. While before Jon's death he may have lived as though Jon and his love would be there forever, the death forced him to see that this was not so. All this called on him to live his life and relationships as authentically as possible. In this sense he saw AIDS

and the devastation it wrought in his life as what awakened him to
a fuller life.

Dave found in AIDS a chance to realize both the importance of
life and the injustice that AIDS engendered. Therefore he saw it as
political as well. "Life is very precarious and you really have got to
appreciate a person while he's around. I guess the only meaning it
had was the injustice that so little is done to find a cure because
it is perceived as a gay disease. There was so much hatred. There
was a woman he [Dave's lover] worked with whom he liked very
much. Her husband, who calls himself a Christian, refused to let her
visit. So, in that sense, I saw the disease as a very political thing."
AIDS brought Dave to see the importance of people, especially those
we love, and of the time we have with them. But it also opened
his eyes to the injustice which AIDS created as it occasioned yet
more expressions of the homophobia which had always been there
in society.

First, there was a lack of interest in finding a cure on the part
of governments, society, and scientists precisely because they viewed
the illness as something which affected gay men exclusively — men
they felt society would be better off without anyway. Second, Dave
saw how individuals could react in very cruel ways to human beings
just because they were gay and because of ignorance of the disease.
He thus saw AIDS as a political reality, one which went beyond the
political and into the moral sphere of justice and love. AIDS could
have a positive meaning in that it made people more aware of life,
but also in that it made people see the underlying evil of prejudice
against fellow human beings. Perhaps some good could come out of
this awful disease if society would take life seriously and attempt
to eradicate the disease of homophobia which gnaws away at our
humanity and compassion.

AIDS: A Positive Experience

For some partners, AIDS has had some explicit positive aspects. In
response to the question about whether AIDS or being HIV positive
might have special meaning, Sloan answered, "Oh, boy, lots. The
positive side has been seeing Keith dealing with it each step along
the way, seeing that he can do it — that it's possible to live with HIV
and with AZT for five years. It's been a positive experience about
what it means to survive. That's the positive side." Seeing someone
with HIV living as fully as possible empowered Sloan with hope,
courage, and increased admiration and love for his partner. He could

face whatever lay in the future as he and Keith lived out their relationship in the context of HIV/AIDS. He still feared being left alone and wondered how he could survive, but he could say that he had found positive meaning in the way that Keith lived with HIV.

Dennis said of the special meaning of AIDS, "It taught me a lot about myself. It showed me that I have personal strengths. It showed me that life can be extraordinarily hard. Situations can be extraordinarily difficult, but if you persevere, things do get better." And Dennis was saying this at a time when he was totally blind due to AIDS complications. His lover had died a few years before after five years of their creating one life. Through the disease and all the ravages it took on him physically and psychologically, he had found an inner strength which he had not suspected existed. This strength brought him to live with AIDS in a very conscious way. Dennis had discovered a meaning which integrated all the elements of his life. He had discovered more fully his spirituality.

AIDS: A Call to Action

If, as we saw above, Dave saw injustice and homophobia surfacing because of AIDS, Frank saw it too, but with a need to change the situation in some way. "Maybe the only meaning it has for me — and more so now — is how much these people need to understand. I guess that has made that feeling in me even stronger now. Because some of the people that should have understood didn't, or were always raising their eyebrows. I think I am going to push, more so than ever, for sick people to have others there to help them." Frank felt determined to make sure that people let go of their fears and lack of understanding so that they would become caregivers for and supporters of those living with HIV/AIDS.

While Cyril did not see any special meaning in AIDS, he noted that it moved him to do things while Louis was still alive. "I felt I had to do in a year what should have taken five years. I wanted to do this and that, to go camping, to take him on trips, to meet his son." Some noted that AIDS got them involved in volunteer work, while others became activists in ACT-UP or other groups. Still others spoke of how they became more conscious of friends who had AIDS and what they could do for them. Whatever it was, people became involved. Action can be anything that contributes to a better life, more quality time for persons living with HIV/AIDS. It can be very public or very private. Whatever enhances life for the lover, the partner, and others, can be the challenge of AIDS.

Greg found that AIDS created a special sensitivity in him. "I've heard people say AIDS was a grace. I don't see AIDS as a grace. I see it as a struggle. I'd have to say I'm more compassionate and more passionate because of that illness. There's a community of survivors that I've become more sensitive to." In Greg, AIDS effected a deeper ability to be with people in their suffering and joys. It made him more "passionate," especially in his determination to right the injustices that persons living with HIV/AIDS endure. He participated in ACT-UP demonstrations. He wrote books affirming gay life and spirituality. He lived as one who cared for others, and AIDS had created this deeper caring that drew on all the talents he had.

AIDS: Bringing People Closer to God

AIDS brought Steve to see God in a different light. In his Native traditions, he had found a God of compassion. He said that AIDS "brought me close to my God. That's the major thing." In his relationship with God, he found strength to open up to others as well. He began to share his status as a person living with HIV rather than hide it as he had done before.

Rick found that Phil's illness brought him to be more understanding of people and to rely on God. "From a spiritual perspective I think you learn to be more tolerant of people's weaknesses and their sufferings. I know that's a cliché, but it's absolutely true. And I see it too as a lesson in faith, at least for myself. And I think for Phil as well. There's a saying that comes to mind: God does not comfort us to make us comfortable but to make us comforters. So I think for myself there are two things. One, it forces me to lean on God. That is one of the things that we all need. He is there, and we're not meant to do it all alone. And again it forces me to lean on friends. It creates an empathy for other people." Finding a deeper relationship with the real God moves us to understand others and their experience in life. Rick spoke of empathy, a sense of being-with the other that is very similar to compassion, which enables us to feel with the other person, especially in suffering. AIDS moved Rick to sense deep within himself that he did not have to go through his experience alone. He saw God with him in all that he faced. He also saw that moving himself out of self-absorption and into relationship with his friends made him more considerate of others. AIDS became for him a challenge to enter community and provide others with the same understanding he had found for himself in God as he and Phil lived out their relationship.

AIDS: No Meaning

Others were adamant in saying that AIDS had no special meaning. While his partner, Sloan, had found much positive meaning in how Keith handled their situation, Keith himself answered that AIDS had no meaning for him.

Harry was unequivocal: "There's no meaning in it. There's no value in it. I said earlier that I believed there are some blessings as a result of the AIDS crisis, but for the individual, I don't know. Meaning? I don't think it means a damned thing. It means you are a creature of nature who is born, who lives for a period of time — in our case, far beyond our natural use. And then finally you break down and die. That's the circle. That's the way it is." Within the cycle of life and death, AIDS becomes simply a part of the natural course of events. Something good may come out of it in general, but for Harry there seemed to be no meaning whatsoever beyond AIDS as a disease affecting the human life process.

Jack stated, "I don't believe that there is any real meaning. It's not for me to question God about the way things are. That belief has come from the Twelve Step Program and my Catholic upbringing." While some might say that Jack's attitude is simple denial, he very sincerely felt that the source of evil events is not the problem. What is important is what we do with them. Jack coped with AIDS by accepting it as part of life. He certainly did not see it as caused by God; this is life, and it is up to us to live as best we can.

Ronald stated quite simply and clearly, "Kerry's illness had no meaning for me, and it has no meaning for all those who are infected."

The partners in this book have taken the step to offer their stories as a liberating potential for other gay men who love men and for all those willing to listen. From their experience they give us hope and advice for living whether as partners of lovers with HIV/AIDS or people in other life contexts. The partners remind those who choose the path of caregiver to do so with love. They note that the commitment requires entering the life of the lover in a new and special way, attempting to see the beautiful, the seemingly little things that might be missed in the horrific times which AIDS may bring. Many also remind us that this is a process which cannot be undergone alone. Help from others can be very practical; it can include providing a break for the caregiving partner or enabling the lovers time to strengthen their bond. It might also mean listening when a partner needs to share what sometimes cannot be shared with the lover. In acknowledging the need for others and for communication with their partners, the partners entered a spiritual path which was concretely enfleshed in each of them individually and as a couple.

Being a couple entails opening the doors to communication. This requires courage and effort. No relationship can grow or survive without the hard work of seeing oneself and the other as authentically as possible. Some partners noted how important it was to continue doing things together in order to share each moment with all its preciousness. Each moment can then become an occasion for embodying as best they can the meaning the partners have found in their shared life.

Some made other observations about life and spirituality, finding something beyond life as we know it, grief as an individual process, and churches which fail to live up to their mission of love. Authentic spirituality is not for these partners an ethereal path, but one that includes the sexual expression of their love as they enflesh the meaning they find in life. For some, the life of love which they lived together created a bond that transcended death, for love never ends. The experience some had of the real presence of their lover after his death enabled them to see the eternity of their love. While churches for the most part did not confirm their loving relationships, some spoke of individual church people who did. Those people became lights for these partners as they journeyed the path to wholeness together.

Can AIDS have a special meaning? For some it was very clear that it meant absolutely nothing. For everyone it was a horrible experience which no human being should have to endure. For others, in retrospect, it became an occasion for learning to appreciate all people and life itself at every instant. For others it became a way to find meaning and to engage themselves in eliminating the injustice and hatred which it brought out in many people. All realized that no meaning could possibly justify the evil which AIDS is for the human community.

The experiences of these partners show us the varying responses to living with a lover who has AIDS. By listening to these stories and noting the partners' determination to love, our world can be enriched.

Conclusion

Living Anew

When we are exploring someone's spirituality, we must first look at that person's life experience. Seeing how people live life in its joys and pains, its elation and sorrow, enables us to determine the elements of their spirituality. Despite a history of dualistic and disembodied notions, spirituality really is down to earth and enfleshed. It is the conscious process of choosing an ultimate value which we then attempt to integrate in a way which opens us to community. As we make this value the core of our lives, our spirituality deepens and we become more fully human. Our lives take on new meaning as we interact with other people, with creation, and with that Power greater than any of us. Spirituality colors everything that is part of our lives. Our sexuality, in all its forms and expressions, is part of the dynamic of spirituality. In relationship, it finds itself enhanced and ever more delightful and expressive of who we are. Spirituality affects all our interactions with others, and we discover how essential the community is for truly human living. As spirituality develops we come to see the world in all its beauty and importance. We affirm our relationship with God or Power or whatever one might name it. The value which we choose to live affects positively and dynamically the persons we are and the experiences we are living.

Our spirituality is nonreligious when it consists of the living out of our chosen ultimate values while we do not belong to an organized religion. For most gay men in relationships, this is perhaps the most common form of spirituality. This is due to the rejection and oppression they experience at the hands of most institutional religions. Some gay men, however, find their place and spirituality within an organized Christian denomination, or in Judaism, Islam, or Buddhism. Whether the spirituality espoused is nonreligious (atheistic or theistic) or religious, when lived out, it can be authentic, valid, and equal to any other. For any authentic spirituality always leads the person to a more fully human existence and is constructive of the human community as a whole.

The gay partners whose stories are told in this book found their spirituality coming alive in their relationships with lovers living with HIV/AIDS. In many ways, their stories are common ones. They met in bars, in schools, at parties, or on dates. Sometimes they were actively looking for a lover. At other times they were looking only for someone to comfort them for the night. For some the relationship took root immediately. For others it took time to develop into commitment. In the steps toward relationship, whether hesitant or firm, we see the beginning of a new lifestyle of love to be colored by new elements in their life together.

As the partners became aware of the seropositive status of their lovers (and sometimes of themselves), all they had desired and planned for in the future seemed to disintegrate. They could not believe what was happening. They feared the other would die. They wondered if there was any future for them at all. This was the beginning of a new stage in their life together. As the disease progressed, the partner found himself preoccupied with worries about the health of his lover. He experienced powerlessness. Even when each experienced the crisis differently, all found themselves moving into an impasse where everything seemed hopeless. What enabled them to get through it was that active surrender to enter fully into whatever their life would hold for them. The partners we have met have lived with deep concern for their lovers, with the determination to be there for the lover. For all, there were times of letting go and of growing, of delightful sharing and anguished fears. The seeming hopelessness of it all nonetheless contained potential for life.

The partners, sometimes consciously, drew on experiences which helped them in caring for their lovers. For some, what they had learned from their families about care for someone you love or for the community as a whole showed them how to live. Others found strength in the faith that God suffered with them and would be there for them. Others had experienced death of family members or previous lovers, and this helped to ground them. With different backgrounds and life experiences, almost all partners found that their ability to care for the lovers up to death was helped by some previous experience in their lives.

As these partners lived their relationships, they discovered or intensified or changed values essential to their lives. Some moved from a fixation on material possessions to desire for a deepening love relationship or to concern for others or the world. For all partners, their loving relationship provided meaning, which affected the whole of their lives. It called them both to see each other as they were. They came through difficult times learning more about the other and about life. Their physical expressions of love became more communicative of who they were and were offering to each other. The meaning they found there constituted the core of their spirituality. Their adherence to that meaning or value was not simply individualistic, but communitarian, since although it began with the couple, it flowed out to the world at large.

To arrive at such a point in their spiritual growth, the partners needed more than each other. We are all constituted by our relationships. Among the most important groups in our lives are our families (both biological and chosen), friends, and religion. In the particular context of gay partners living with HIV/AIDS, each of these groups takes on a particular significance.

A family is more than just a group of individuals who have the same blood lines. What constitutes the core of a family is what it offers to the person. At its best, family offers us a sense of security and freedom to be ourselves. Family is where we are at home. But without the nurturing care, understanding, and support, family does not exist for the individual. Only when the physical elements of family join together with its *spiritual* elements to create a place of real safety, growth, freedom, and maturity can we speak of family. When gay men in our society come out to their families, they can discover that they really do have families in this deepest sense. Or they might find that they do not. Some find support and encouragement immediately. Some find it over a period of time, as "family" members struggle with their socially constructed views of homosexuality. Others never find it at all as they are rejected immediately and consistently by their "family." We have seen all these types of familial relationships as the partners' stories unfolded.

We have also seen how several partners spoke of *families of choice*. Some whose biological families had rejected them spoke of the key role their families of choice played in providing them with a safe place to be and to live. These families of choice were composed of friends who spent time together, allowing and encouraging positive characteristics in each other as they played together, laughed together, and cried together. Such families of choice incarnate what it really means to be family. They are essential in our society, for none of us can become authentically who we are without the security zone of family. When the biological family never develops into a real family, the family of choice becomes absolutely necessary. Even when the biological family is authentically family, very often gay men and lesbians seek out families of choice to provide what even the best of biological families might not be able to provide due to distance or societal difficulties. They do this also because of the innate need to relate positively to people who are also gay or are gay positive. Nor is it unusual for nongay people to have families of choice as well, especially when they are from dysfunctional families or live at a physical distance from their own families.

Closely associated with (and often part of) families of choice are friends. From our childhood days we seek out friends, those with whom we can be intimate and share our innermost thoughts. These are people with whom we can be ourselves and know that we will be loved. They are the people we love in such a way that they too realize they are safe to be themselves and to develop into fully human beings. In friendship is the foundation for human community. Friends are particularly important for gay men whose lovers live with HIV/AIDS. They provide the support necessary to continue and deepen their relationship within the context of disease. Their homes are places of peace and laughter, their dinners eucharistic meals at which more than physical bread is shared. With friends, the gay festive seasons become liturgical seasons of gathering and celebrating common bonds in special ways. The partners spoke of how HIV/AIDS showed them who their real friends were. Some were surprised at who actually were their steadfast friends. For all, friendship provided not only the support they needed, but an environment which opened the potential for a healthy human life as well as an ever-deepening spirituality.

While some partners could not affirm any God, most spoke of the God they had found. The stories of God which these partners told were stories of an *incarnate* God. They had no need or desire for a God out of this world. Theirs was a God who not only loved them as they were as gay men and lovers, but who suffered with them in painful times and laughed with them in good times. There was a certain familiarity with this God they envisaged as enjoying to be with them, especially in their love for each other as couples. Their God may not have all the neatness of a religious dogma or a formal theological statement, but what each one said concerning God was definitely theology. It was their faith seeking understanding. Their affirmations of God with them were authentic affirmations of their continuing faith which constantly had to battle the condemnations which most religions would foist upon them and their views. It was upon their notions of God that they established their communication with God — prayer.

For them, prayer became a conversation with God. Very often it was informal. It involved listening as well as speaking, or simply being with God when one was totally exhausted, or filled with boisterous energy, distraught, hopeless, or overflowing with possibility. The conversation of prayer takes place in many forms. As the lovers turn to God, they might ask for better health or no pain. They might thank God for the good days and the love they are experiencing. Prayer might take the form of making love or actually living life. The partners affirmed that God was in the midst of their lovemaking, their bodies entwined in delight. Prayer was for them a *con-versatio*, a turning together with God in life based upon a conversation, a sharing of reality. As such it was a *com-unio*, a union with each other *in this life, this world*.

Through their relationships the partners had experience to share with others who might be going through very similar events. To live in relationship with someone living with HIV/AIDS requires committing oneself to caregiving. This is extremely difficult and can wear one down physically and emotionally. It is important for caregivers to seek friends or volunteers to provide respite for the partner caring for his lover, but also so that the lovers can have time together as friends to take care of tasks that would otherwise have occupied the partner. In the time they have, the lovers should live life and communicate as much as possible with each other. It is particularly important for the partner to be open to the little things, the beauty of their lover or some particular situation.

Can AIDS have a special meaning? Only those who live intimately with it can answer that question. And once again, the answer will be influenced by the individual's life experience, his story. The partners spoke of its meaning in a variety of ways. Some spoke of the experience of living with AIDS as a positive experience — in retrospect. These saw the experience leading them to love more deeply than they might have done without the presence of AIDS. Others felt that it taught them the value of all things and all people. Some spoke of it as a call to do something constructive, something which would affect the life of the human community positively. Still others spoke of it as bringing them closer to God. For some, it had no meaning whatsoever. Its destructiveness and the anguish it brought to all those involved remained too great to see it in a positive light.

What we have seen throughout the unfolding of these stories of men and their lovers who live with HIV/AIDS is how they found life in a context which seems utterly opposed to life. As they lived each moment with evident love, they were living a spirituality which provided meaning for them. That spirituality developed over time in a variety of circumstances, not the least of which was living with HIV/AIDS.

— ◆ —

If there is anything we can learn about spirituality from these stories, it is that spirituality is indeed an enfleshed reality. The common view that spirituality is totally otherworldly no longer can be maintained. The historical split between body and spirit is unacceptable. The human being is not a spirit (or soul) imprisoned in a body whose only task is to weigh it down and keep it from soaring into the spirit universe. We are persons whose lives are to be lived in the flesh-and-blood realities that we are. Jesus offered us the only way to be fully human and thus fully spiritual. That was the way of love. The love of which he spoke was not an ethereal love that is unaware of, or suspicious of, the body. Jesus' advocacy of love meant that he realized and wanted all persons to dwell in this world and enjoy the blessings of incarnatedness, of sensuality, and of wholeness. For him, love can transform the world — not into a heavenly place of spirits — but into a positive, sensual life of relationships. To live the life of God meant, for Jesus, to live this life *now*. To love another is to open oneself to the mystery of life and its sacredness. It is to give oneself to the other in full delight and the pleasure of being in relation to the other. In the other's response of self-giving, the lover and the beloved become one in a life where mystery finds flesh. This love which is intensely and passionately physical is at the same time intensely and passionately spiritual. For it is only in the ecstatic wonder of our bodiliness that mystery comes alive in and for us. By affirming and living in love which moves us out of self to other, we are living our spirituality. Fundamentally, the ultimate value which provides the meaning of life for the individual is the same for all — love.

It is love that attracts us. Desirous as we all are for true union with another, love provides not only the way to that union but it provides us with the enhancement of that union. Love is the motivating force that moves each person in the human community to truly live. It sees and affirms the unique treasure of every human being. But more than that, love empowers us to make of the world the place of God, the home of God. We begin by being drawn out of ourselves to another whom we love and desire. The union which the two thereby establish in passionate love moves them to concern and love for the human community. In a variety of ways, the two in love create the possibility for love to spread through our human community more and more. For none of us is indeed alone, and our becoming is accomplished in our interaction and relationship with the community. In that love which lovers share comes a deep concern for the earth. For we come to realize in love that everything we are is essentially connected with nature, the ground of our lives. The deeper and the more passionate the love one has for the other, the more we see the incredible unity of all things and all being in the mystery and sacredness of life.

The gay men who live passionately as lovers within the context of HIV/AIDS and whose stories are shared here have found that key of love and unity. They are not saints—if one envisions saints as characters living out of this world. But they are saints if one sees saints as people who live and love passionately, each in their own way, place, and time. For those partners who were believers, the heart of this passionate love was a God who lived all that life has to offer with them. Theirs was a God of life *now*. For those who were not believers, the heart of their passionate love was life in all its mystery and sacredness. It was life lived *now*.

Perhaps the gift of gay men in this century is to offer the whole human community an authentic way of living spirituality. Rejected because of being different from the majority, gay men have to live many losses—family, friends, careers, even religion. But rather than allowing these losses to destroy them or define them or cause them to remain inauthentic, the gay men whose stories we have heard dare to affirm their innate goodness. They have had the courage to live honestly and humanly the love which life has given them. When passion and sensuality are condemned by others, these gay men affirm the fundamental wonder and goodness of human passion and sensuality. By so doing and by so living, they offer a challenge to the human community at large and to the Christian churches in particular to reexamine life and see the goodness of all that is. They integrate in a variety of ways the core values of human life. In doing so, each one offers a very special gift to the humanization of the world and ultimately to making the world into the home of God who is Life.

Notes

Introduction

1. Paul Monette, *Borrowed Time: An AIDS Memoir* (San Diego: Harcourt Brace Jovanovich, 1986).

2. Paul Monette, *Love Alone: Eighteen Elegies for Rog* (New York: Harrington Park Press, 1995).

3. Joe Brown, ed., *A Promise to Remember: The Names Project Book of Letters: Remembrances from the Contributors to the Quilt* (New York: Avon Books, 1992).

4. Neal Hitchens, ed., *Voices That Care: Stories and Encouragements for People with AIDS/HIV and Those Who Love Them* (New York: Simon & Schuster, 1992).

5. R. Dennis Shelby, *If a Partner Has AIDS: Guide to Clinical Intervention for Relationships in Crisis* (New York: Harrington Park Press, 1992). See also his later book, *People with HIV and Those Who Help Them* (New York: Harrington Park Press, 1995), esp. 129–31.

6. Robert J. L. Publicover, *My Unicorn Has Gone Away: Life, Death, Grief, and Living in the Years of AIDS* (Somerville, Mass.: Powder House Publishing, 1992).

7. Mark Doty, *Heaven's Coast: A Memoir* (New York: HarperCollins Publishers, 1996); Fenton Johnson, *Geography of the Heart: A Memoir* (New York: Scribner, 1996).

Chapter 1: Spirituality

8. Kate Kendell, "Out in Front: A Faustian Choice," in *San Francisco Frontiers News Magazine* 16, no. 9 (August 28, 1997): 35.

9. See Michael Callen's *Surviving AIDS* (New York: HarperCollins Publishers, 1990), which provides some first-hand reflections on the spirituality of gay men who live with HIV/AIDS. See especially the statements of "A. J." Roosevelt Williams statements (111) and of Ron (160–61). See also Robert Barzan, ed., *Sex and Spirit: Exploring Gay Men's Spirituality* (San Francisco: White Crane Newsletter, 1995), which contains chapters reflecting on a variety of spiritualities espoused by gay men. Also see Tom Moon, "The Examined Life: A Gay Spiritual Sensibility," in *San Francisco Frontiers News Magazine* 16, no. 14 (November 6, 1997): 32, where he speaks of groups of gay persons trying to live a specifically gay spirituality in San Francisco and the characteristics of that spirituality.

10. For an excellent presentation of the history of the term see Walter Principe, "Toward Defining 'Spirituality,'" in *Studies in Religion/Sciences Religieuses* 12, no. 2 (Spring 1983): 127–41.

11. Certainly there were people, even clergy, who did not think this way, but the dualism which had infected Christianity took its toll among the majority of clergy and believers, who then felt they had to deny the body and worldly things if they were to attain that goal of eternity. Such a view, however, had no foundation in the life and teachings of the historical Jesus of Nazareth upon whom Christianity was to be based. This false dualism was really the result of early Greek philosophers whose thought processes entered the Christian sphere as early as Augustine of Hippo in the fourth and fifth centuries.

12. See Richard P. Hardy, "Living Spirituality: The Essence of Being Human," in *CHAC Review* 24, no. 2 (Summer 1996): 3–7. Also Daniel A. Helminiak, *The Human Core of Spirituality: Mind as Psyche and Spirit* (Albany: State University Press of New York, 1996), esp. 233–67.

13. See the excellent chapter by Michael L. Stemmeler, "Empowerment: The Construction of Gay Religious Identities," in Bjorn Krondorfer, ed., *Men's Bodies, Men's Gods: Male Identities in a (Post-)Christian Culture* (New York: New York University Press, 1996), 94–107.

14. See the chapter "Gay Fecundity or Liberating Sexuality" in André Guindon, *The Sexual Creators: An Ethical Proposal for Concerned Christians* (Lanham, Md.: University Press of America, 1986), 117–58. For the notion of being "from the margins," I am indebted to Daniel T. Spencer, *Gay and Gaia: Ethics, Ecology and the Erotic* (Cleveland: Pilgrim Press, 1996).

15. Mark Doty, *Heaven's Coast: A Memoir* (New York: HarperCollins Publishers, 1996), 286–87.

16. Fenton Johnson, *Geography of the Heart: A Memoir* (New York: Scribner, 1996), 226.

17. Peter H. Van Ness, ed., *Spirituality and the Secular Quest*, World Spirituality: An Encyclopedic History of the Religious Quest 22 (New York: Crossroad Publishing Company, 1996), 2.

18. Ibid., 5 and 7.

19. This does not mean that there is no place for celibacy in a particular human life and even in a particular gay man's life. When chosen for a positive, healthy reason, celibacy is and can be life-fulfilling, but only if it is chosen as a way to wholeness; and not out of fear either of sex or religious condemnation of one's sexual expression. Some gay men do find celibacy — either temporarily or as a whole lifestyle — as *their* path to wholeness which does not deny their sexuality and their gayness. For a short but interesting article on the subject see Robert L. Pela, "Sexless (but Not Loveless) Marriages," in *Genre* 46 (March 1997): 60–63. An excellent academic presentation on celibacy is to be found in André Guindon, "Celibate Fecundity or Recreating Communities," in *The Sexual Creators*, 205–34.

20. See Helminiak, *The Human Core of Spirituality*, 244. See also p. 248, where he speaks of "sex just for fun," noting how this expression of sexuality can be "an instance of caring and interpersonal relating."

21. We will see how the partners who shared their stories of love in this book found their intimate relationship with their lover a profound challenge leading to the realization of the oneness which all human beings can find with all that

exists. Their love, both emotional and physical, moved them to that discovery and life.

22. See Thich Nhat Hanh, *Peace Is Every Step: The Path of Mindfulness in Everyday Life* (New York: Bantam Books, 1992).

23. Daniel A. Helminiak, "Non-Religious Lesbians and Gays Facing AIDS: A Fully Psychological Approach to Spirituality," in *Pastoral Psychology* 43, no. 5 (1995): 307.

24. Sandra M. Schneiders, "Theology and Spirituality: Strangers, Rivals, or Partners," in *Horizons* 13, no. 2 (1986): 266.

25. Michael Downey, *Understanding Christian Spirituality* (Mahwah, N.J.: Paulist Press, 1997), 35. See also the Anglican priest Kenneth Leech, *The Eye of the Storm: Living Spirituality in the Real World* (San Francisco: HarperSan-Francisco, 1992), esp. 215–39, where he reflects upon key points which he sees in a renewed Christian spirituality.

26. Leech, *The Eye of the Storm*, emphasizes throughout the incarnated core of Christian spirituality.

27. Whether or not Schneiders or others would agree, I maintain that a Christian spirituality without specific church membership is clearly possible, providing that it is lived in relation to a community of others who believe in Jesus Christ. Thus, it is possible for a gay man who has rejected or been rejected by the institutional church to still find his ultimate value in the God made known in Jesus Christ in the Spirit as he lives intimately with his lover and within the community. He may create his own symbols and rituals which actualize and express his belief and find all aspects of his life permeated and enhanced by that belief — even his sexuality and physical lovemaking. While such a religious spirituality is not the only option for the gay man, it can be an *option* and a very constructive one at that. Each gay man needs to reflect on his story and his life and find that core value which involves him in a process of integration to wholeness.

28. See the very fine study by J. Michael Clark, *Beyond Our Ghettos: Gay Theology in Ecological Perspective* (Cleveland: Pilgrim Press, 1993), in which he speaks of the opening out of the gay community to ecological concerns and why it must be this way. See as well Spencer's *Gay and Gaia*.

29. See the Second Vatican Council's document *Dogmatic Constitution on Divine Revelation*, no. 2.

Chapter 2: To Meet for a Lifetime

30. There have been stories of high school men deciding to attend a prom together or university students deciding to attend a special event as a male couple. The very fact, however, that these stories occupy the media's attention shows that they are the exception and that these men are exceptional. The struggle which teenagers have in integrating their gay identities in a hostile world remains, and we see it in the high number of suicides of gay and lesbian teens. For one poignant story see Leroy Aarons, *Prayers for Bobby: A Mother's Coming to Terms with the Suicide of Her Gay Son* (San Francisco: HarperSanFrancisco, 1995).

31. See John E. Fortunato, *Embracing the Exile: Healing Journeys of Gay Christians* (San Francisco: HarperSanFrancisco, 1982).

32. I am convinced that in a society free of homophobia many of these negative elements would disappear as gay people could be who they are and find the support necessary, thus developing into whole and healthy human beings. In his book on homophobia Blumenfeld shows how everyone, gay and straight, pays the price of homophobia. Removing homophobia would not create a perfect society. Yet it is a necessary step which would lead to development and human progress for all. See Warren J. Blumenfeld, ed., *Homophobia: How We All Pay the Price* (Boston: Beacon Press, 1992).

33. "Counsels to a Religious on How to Reach Perfection," no. 3, 726, in *The Collected Works of St. John of the Cross,* trans. Kieran Kavanaugh and Otilio Rodriguez (Washington, D.C.: ICS Publications, 1991).

34. At the time of the interview, Jerry was alive though having some minor physical problems.

35. In fact, Stan took care of his ex-lover for the last six month's of his ex-lover's life.

36. At the time of the interview, they had been together for about six years.

Chapter 3: Crisis: Risks and Opportunity

37. This is often the case for partners. David expresses it well when he speaks of the situation with his partner Mark: "There was nothing you could do.... There were times when I thought it would be better for all of us if he died. There were times when it seemed very close and it was almost a relief. Then he would spring back a bit and we were happy about that. Then, it would start all over again.... I guess I expected a kind of linear order, and that's how I prepared myself. I guess the biggest stress was that things keep bouncing back and forth, and you can't prepare. It's the fact that you can't prepare yourself. I felt constantly on the edge."

38. Augustine of Hippo, *The Confessions of St. Augustine,* trans. with introduction and notes by John K. Ryan (Garden City, N.Y.: Image Books, 1960), book 4, chap. 6, p. 100. This section of his *Confessions* makes it quite clear that Augustine and his friend had a homosexual relationship.

39. Very often partners spoke specifically of their concern for the other. Jack said of Jerry, "I want to provide for him the best health care I can. What also preoccupies me is concern about his health. I always ask how he's feeling. Every morning I ask him how he slept.... At the least sign of anything I'll think, 'Oh, my God, is this the beginning — what if he dies?' Occasionally, I get those thoughts, but it's more of a concern in terms of 'Am I doing everything I can to help him?'" Each partner gave of himself for the sake of the other. Later we will see how they often found that they needed to take time off or in some other way care for themselves if they were to be able to continue to care for their lovers.

40. Tim was alive, though ill, at the time of the interview. Subsequently, they held a ceremony of commitment, traveled some, and enjoyed each other's company until Tim's death a few months later.

41. See André Guindon, *The Sexual Language: An Essay in Moral Theology* (Ottawa: University of Ottawa Press, 1976), and *Sexual Creators: An Ethical Proposal for Concerned Christians* (Lanham, Md.: University Press of America, 1986).

42. Dennis said, "I think the most difficult part was keeping the secret just between the two of us and being so afraid it would be disclosed — that somebody would figure it out. We worried about the repercussions that would come out of that. In the early '80s people were more afraid of AIDS than they are now."

43. See Mark Doty, *Heaven's Coast: A Memoir* (New York: HarperCollins Publishers, 1996), 221ff.

44. Frank found that physical changes in his partner, Fabian, created problems for both of them. The difficulties began "I guess... when the KS started. The difficulty I had was the sadness of seeing him react to every little mark he saw. He would say 'This has got to be KS. We've got to get this checked out.'"

45. Duane's partner, Bruce, was still alive at the time of the interview.

46. Jake spoke in a similar way saying, "There were obviously changes that occurred as he got sicker. During the last couple of years, I couldn't plan anything. I couldn't plan vacations. I couldn't plan events because I never knew when he was going to get sick... so I felt like we were at the mercy of the illness."

47. Claude and Shaun were positive at the time of the interview and were interviewed together. Claude was always worried about his health — they jokingly spoke of him as a hypochondriac. But they were a couple who were well matched. Claude said, "You know in our relationship, I'm stronger in some ways, but when it regards illness, he is stronger than I am, and that's a good mix. I feel you [looking at Shaun] are very much more supportive that way. I know I can count on him." Later in the interview, Shaun noted that when the crunch came, he could and would take care of Claude. The weeks Claude was in the hospital, Shaun was there talking with the doctors, the social workers, getting things settled. Shaun's parents were there too, sitting with Claude when Shaun had to be away.

48. Duncan too found at one point that he could not care for Cliff at home anymore. Cliff's doctor tried to dissuade Duncan from bringing Cliff in to the hospital, but Duncan was determined. "Mentally, he just wasn't present.... It wasn't just taking care of diapers. ...I mean I had to restrain him. I had to watch him completely and I couldn't do that. I just thought, 'I've had it.' There was anger frustration, pain, sadness — a whole gamut of feelings. Depression."

49. Rico reached a point of total frustration trying to care for Jon at home, yet he wanted to keep him there and care for him. He went to a center for help, feeling totally unable to handle the situation alone. The social workers suggested he put Jon in a hospice or some similar facility. "Finally, I said, 'All I want is more help. Give me more help.' So they did. And still it wasn't enough." Yet Rico endured, and he says that he was able to because of Jon himself. "His smile, his appreciation, his trust. All these little things. I saw a beauty, and from the beginning I really made an effort to make the best of the whole situation."

Chapter 4: Values and Development

50. See John E. Fortunato, *Embracing the Exile: Healing Journeys of Gay Christians* (San Francisco: HarperSanFrancisco, 1982); this whole book is based upon this theme.

51. In *The Sexual Creators: An Ethical Proposal for Concerned Christians* (Lanham, Md.: University Press of America, 1986), André Guindon uses the paradigm of language to speak of sexuality. He notes how we all have to learn to speak a language and the very process involves making mistakes. The same holds true for sexuality and our process of living it out in a healthy fashion. We will make mistakes, but these can enable us to learn how to speak the sexual language more authentically as life develops and our story unfolds.

52. Duncan died a few months after the interview, of complications from AIDS. At his memorial service, the eulogy given by his friend and the homily given by the priest underlined the importance of relationships and concern for others which permeated his life.

53. After Karl died, Jason worked for an Asian AIDS service group. About six months before the interview took place, he had his first AIDS marking complication and was thinking of going on disability, but various experiences helped him to decide that it wasn't the time yet.

54. For others like Chris, the important things remained the same as well. He noted though that "the sexual aspect of our relationship was limited at best [during Phil's illness] and gradually nonexistent.... Yet the devotion and commitment to do good, to be honest, and sincere were there."

55. Mario died a short time before the interview, and Stan was still in an intense grieving period. Doing the interview was important for him.

56. R. Dennis Shelby describes some of the difficulties raised by HIV/AIDS in a relationship in his book *People with HIV and Those Who Help Them* (New York: Harrington Park Press, 1996), 129–31.

Chapter 5: Communities of Support

57. For more detail on "families of choice" see Kath Weston, *Families We Choose: Lesbians, Gays, Kinship* (New York: Columbia University Press, 1991). See also Stanley Siegel and Ed Lowe, Jr., *Unchartered Lives: Understanding the Life Passages of Gay Men* (New York: Penguin Books, Dutton, 1994), 158ff. Robert Goss and Amy Adams Squires Stronghart are editors of a book which speaks of the varieties of families found within the gay community, *Our Families, Our Values: Snapshots of Queer Kinship* (New York: Haworth Press, 1997).

58. Mario was the eldest of the boys in a very large family whose father had left them. He felt it was his duty to stay and take care of them. So Mario supported the whole family until he was thirty-nine years old.

59. The new drug combination treatments seem to be having results unthought of just a few years ago. In the long run, they may or may not break through the cycle of death which we have been experiencing through the decimation of our community since the outbreak of the epidemic in North America.

60. See Walt Odets, *In the Shadow of the Epidemic: Being HIV-Negative in the Age of AIDS* (Durham, N.C.: Duke University Press, 1995).

Chapter 6: Images of God and Prayer

61. *The Ascent of Mount Carmel*, book 2, chap. 22, par. 5 in *The Collected Works of St. John of the Cross*, trans. Kieran Kavanaugh and Otilio Rodriguez (Washington, D.C.: ICS Publications, 1991), 230–31.

62. *The Sayings of Light and Love*, no. 60, in *The Collected Works of St. John of the Cross*, 90.

63. See the superb reflections of gay men on religion and faith in Brian Bouldrey, ed., *Wrestling with the Angel: Faith and Religion in the Lives of Gay Men* (New York: Riverhead Books, 1995).

64. See the work by Larry Dossey, *Healing Words: The Power of Prayer and the Practice of Meditation* (San Francisco: HarperSanFrancisco, 1993).

65. Various images of God in the context of AIDS are reflected upon theologically by Ronald Nicolson, *God in AIDS? A Theological Enquiry* (London: SCM Press, 1996), 24–29.

66. See Barbara Bozak's chapter "Speech for the Speechless, Power for the Powerless," in Normand Bonneau, Barbara Bozak, André Guindon, and Richard P. Hardy, *AIDS and Faith* (Ottawa: Novalis, 1993), 39–58.

Chapter 7: Sharing Hope: Some Advice

67. An excellent resource for caregiving at home is found in Andrew S. Johnson, *Living with Dying: Dying at Home: An AIDS Care Team Resource Manual* (Toronto: AIDS Committee of Toronto — ACT). While situations differ in various provinces of Canada and states in the United States, in Ontario, the partner, by law, has precedence in making medical treatment decisions over parents and families. Unfortunately, not many other places are as enlightened in this area.